Ambedkar Marathwada University, Aurangabad, Dr. A. P. Borade and Prof. A. D. Godase for inspiring me to complete this book.

I thank my father Prakash Bholane, mother Sunanda Bholane, brother Vaibhav Bholane and father-in-law Gangadhar Sohani for their love, guidance and for always believing

And, finally I am grateful to my loving and understanding wife Manjushree and my sweet son Atharva for their patience, love, encouragement and sacrifices.

Dr. Kishor P. Bholane

INDEX

Chapter No.	Name of the Chapter	Page No.
I	Introduction	1
II	Researches Relating to the Job Satisfaction	7
III	Researches Relating to the Job Involvement	32
IV	Researches Relating to the Organizational Commitment	44
V	Researches Relating to the Relationship between Job Satisfaction and Job Involvement	67
VI	Researches Relating to the Relationship between Job Satisfaction and Organizational Commitment	75
VII	Researches Relating to the Relationship between Job Involvement and Organizational Commitment	100

PREFACE

Every organization has four most important elements man, money, method and material. Out of these, the single most important element is human being. This operates the other three in such a way that the organization may achieve its goals. Workforce is the most important factor and the only sustainable long-term competitive advantage of an organization.

Employees are one of the most important determinants and leading factors that determine the success of an organization in a competitive environment. This is especially true for service organizations that rely heavily on their good behavioural employees to provide friendly and courteous services to their customers in this competitive environment. With increase in competition firms have recognized importance of employee's satisfaction and performance and are developing their human resource capital to compete in this global market. Job satisfaction, job involvement and organizational commitment in organizations have been receiving increasing attention because they reduce employee turnover, absenteeism, tardiness, and health setbacks due to stress. The effectiveness and productivity of an organization depends on the development and nurturing of its staff. It is neither possible nor practical to increase the productivity of an organization without considering the optimal exploiting of the staff's capabilities.

Previous researchers have concluded that employees are the real assets for the organizations, and to satisfy customers, organizations must satisfy their employee's requirements. Customer's satisfaction and organizations performance is the result of its employee's satisfaction.

To cope with increased competitive pressure, globalization and demand for efficiency, many organizations have come to rely on the strategy of restructuring and downsizing. The effectiveness of this strategy, however, depends, in part, on its impact on survivors' work attitudes and behaviors. Unfortunately, much of the evidence from research on survivors' work-related attitudes and behaviors subsequent to restructuring and downsizing have documented evidence decline in job satisfaction, job involvement and organizational commitment.

A better understanding of the complex relationships between job satisfaction, job involvement and organizational commitment of employees will result in practical benefits for organizations, with a particular emphasis on creating positive environment at work. This book may be helpful to the researchers to find out the under researched areas in the field of job satisfaction, job involvement and organizational commitment.

I express my deep sense of gratitude and respect to Dr. J. R. Suryawanshi, Professor, Department of Commerce, Dr. Babasaheb

CHAPTER – I

INTRODUCTION

For any investigation in any field of knowledge extensive use of the library and thorough investigation of related literature and references are essential. The study and investigation of related literature is a time consuming affair but it is a very fruitful phase of a research programme. Each investigator must have adequate knowledge of the sources of his problem area and also must know what has already been discovered relating to his field. He must not only be adequately familiar with the sources to use but he must also know where and how find them. This knowledge will go a long way to help him to save many hours of aimless activity. Thus the review of related literature as well as research implies the regarding, surveying and evaluating of the written form of literature related to the problem area which is available in libraries and from many sources. Writing about the importance of the review of related literature John W. Best states, "The search for reference materials is a time consuming, but fruitful phase of the graduate program. A familiarity with the literature in any problem area helps the students to discover what is already known, what others have attempted to find out, what methods have been promising or disappointing and what problems remain to be solved."

Borg says "The review of the literature in educational research provides one with means of getting to the frontier in a particular field". According to Borg, the survey of related literature enables an investigator in such a manner as he can discover what has already not been investigated and evaluated.[1]

Thus a review of the literature is a very important aspect of research work. It provides not only information only the status of knowledge in the area one intends to study but also points out deficiencies in available research works and provides direction for the design one may eventually use in conducting his research. In this book an author has tried to focus light on the research studies done so far on the job attitudes namely, job satisfaction, job involvement and organizational commitment.

Job satisfaction is how people feel about their jobs and different aspects of their jobs.[2] Job satisfaction is the extent to which employees like their work.[3] Job satisfaction occurs when attributes of the job comply with the demands of the worker and the worker is pleased with his job. Job satisfaction is a set of favorable or unfavorable feelings and emotion with which employees view their works. Employees experiencing high satisfaction levels contribute to organizational commitment, improved physical and mental health, and improved quality of life both on and off the job. Job dissatisfaction on the other hand, culminates in higher absenteeism, turnover, labour problems, labour grievances, attempts to organise labour unions and a negative organizational climate.[4]

Job involvement refers to how people perceive their jobs in relation to (i) the working environment, (ii) the job itself, and (iii) how their work and life are integrated.[5] Having low involvement contributes to employees' feelings of alienation of purpose, alienation in the organisation or feeling of separation between what the employees see as their "life" and the job they do. In short, job involvement refers to the extent to which an individual identifies with his job, actively participates in it and considers his performance important to self-worth.

Organizational commitment is defined as psychological state that binds the individual to the organization.[6] Organizational commitment is the degree to which an employee identifies with a particular organisation and its goals, and wishes to maintain membership in the organisation.[7] There is much research suggesting that organizational commitment leads to, or is associated with variables of great importance for organizational success and efficiency – or lack thereof – such as absenteeism, labour turnover and productivity.

Human behavior plays a significant role in maximizing organizational effectiveness, regardless of technological development.

An individual who has high level of job satisfaction holds positive attitudes towards the job. Workers who are satisfied at their workplaces show positive attitudes in their homes and make a psychologically healthy society. Understanding job satisfaction is critical to the success of an organization. Any effort to maximize organizational effectiveness requires a higher degree of job involvement among members of an organization.[8] An individual with a high level of job involvement is likely to be highly satisfied, more productive and less prone to leave than the one with a low level of job involvement. That is, job involvement is an important motivational variable for any organization. Organizational commitment directly affects employees' performance and is therefore treated as an issue of great importance.[9] Highly committed individual is more likely to be a better performer is less prone to resign than the one with a low level of organizational commitment.

REFERENCES

1) Ambhore D. S. (2011). A comparative study of anxiety, adjustment and achievement motivation of tribal and non-tribal girls in Nandurbar district. A Ph. D. thesis, Dr. Babasaheb Ambedkar Marathwada University, Aurangabad, p. 82.

2) Spector P.E. (1997). Job satisfaction: Application, assessment, causes and consequences. Harper & Row, New York, p. 96.

3) Ellickson M. C. & Logsdon K. (2002). Determinants of job satisfaction of municipal government employees [Electronic version]. Public Personnel Management, Vol. 31(3), pp. 343-358.

4) Cherrington D. J. (1994). Organizational behavior (2nd Ed.). Allyn and Bacon Inc., Boston, p. 112.

5) Hisrchfeld R. R. & Field H. S. (2000). Work centrality and work alienation: Distinct aspects of a general commitment to work. Journal of Organizational Behavior, Vol. 21(7), pp. 789-800.

6) Allen N. J. & Meyer J. P. (1990). The measurement and antecedents of affective, continuance and normative commitment to the organization. Journal of Occupational Psychology, Vol. 63 (1), pp. 1-18.

7) Robbins S. P. (1998). Organizational behavior. (8th Ed.). Prentice Hall, New Jersey, p. 142.

8) Elankumaran S. (2004). Personality, organizational climate and job involvement: An empirical study. Journal of Human Values, Vol. 10, pp. 117-130.

9) Vijayashree L. & Jagdischchandra M. V. (2011). Locus of control and job satisfaction: PSU employees. Serbian Journal of Management, Vol. 6(2), pp. 193-203.

CHAPTER – II

RESEARCHES RELATING TO THE JOB SATISFACTION

Bronski D. C. and Cook S. (1994) interviewed 334 Ohayo University graduate physicians. For the interviews, they used Job Discriminative Index questionnaire, in which satisfaction is assessed according to five sub-scales (work, co-workers, management, current reward and promotion opportunities). The research showed that job satisfaction is not directly related to practical aspects of physicians.[1]

Okerlund V. W., Jacson P. B. and Parsons R. J. (1994) research revealed that Utah physicians were satisfied with their job. Respondents indicated the followings factors as the most important and having the greatest effect on their job satisfaction: working freedom, assistance in skills development, and salary and fringe benefits. The survey also showed that the key factors of doctors' willingness to leave their practice comprised such things as big clerical workload, dissatisfaction with reforms, high patient expectations and big clinical workload. While young doctors willing to leave practice mainly emphasised communication problems and big clinical workload, older doctors were mainly discontent with changes in the health care system and big clerical workload. Differences between genders were insignificant.[2]

Speakman C. B., Pleasant J. M. and Sutton G.B. (1996) conducted a study of 106 Texas (USA) doctors' job satisfaction. Respondents stated that their work was a challenge in a positive sense: it enabled them to use their capabilities and was stimulating. The doctors also pointed out that they were given sufficient autonomy at work and independence in decision-making, and were able to learn and improve their work. The doctors, however, were dissatisfied with the clerical aspect of their work.[3]

Khan M. A. (1999) compared job satisfaction among teachers of government and private secondary schools in Karachi. The reason for comparison of the two sets of teachers, one in the government sector and other in the private sector was to bring into focus the degree of variation in job satisfaction experienced by the teachers working in two quantitatively different work environments. The population of the study consisted of all secondary school teachers in Karachi. The total sample size was 300 teachers. Stratified random sampling technique was used for collecting data. This study showed that there was a significant difference between the government and private secondary school teachers of Karachi in their mean scores of job satisfaction. It was clear that the private secondary school teachers were more satisfied with their jobs than the government secondary school teachers in Karachi. The private secondary school teachers were more satisfied with their jobs relating to the physiological needs and social needs than the government secondary school teachers, whereas government secondary school teachers were more satisfied with their jobs relating to the professional needs, economical needs and esteem needs.[4]

Murray R. A. (1999) investigated job satisfaction of professional and paraprofessional library staff at the University Of North Carolina at Chapel Hill. The survey was distributed in November 1998 to the 240 permanent staff employed by the UNC-Chapel Hill Academic Affairs Library at that time. Of that number, 89 surveys were sent to professional librarians and 151 were sent to paraprofessional staff. One hundred forty-five completed surveys were returned for a response rate of 60.4%. Of these, 59 were returned by professional librarians and 86 by paraprofessionals, making the response rate for the two groups 66.3% and 57.0% respectively. The results of this study indicated that employees at the Academic Affairs Library of the University of North Carolina at Chapel Hill are satisfied with their jobs. Professionals were significantly more satisfied than paraprofessionals in the areas of enjoyment of the work itself, coworkers, appreciation, promotion, pay and overall satisfaction.[5]

Brewer E. W. and Landers J. M. (2003) investigated job satisfaction among industrial and technical teacher educators. The population for the study consisted of industrial and technical teacher educators in the United States. The Industrial Teacher Education Directory provided the sampling frame. Using purely random procedures, the researchers drew a sample of 347 from the

1,752 industrial and technical teacher educators (excluding department heads, coordinators, and other administrators) identified in the Directory. Of the 347 questionnaires sent to the sample, 133 were returned, for a response rate of 38.3%. The majority of respondents were male (84.5%). Results from the *t*-tests indicated that the sample from this study reported significantly more satisfaction ($p < 0.001$) with promotion and nature of work and significantly less satisfaction ($p < 0.001$) with operating conditions than did the norm sample. No significant predictors were found for the job satisfaction facets of supervision, coworkers, nature of work, and communication. Significant predictors were found for pay, promotion, benefits, contingent rewards, operating conditions, and overall job satisfaction.[6]

Michalinos Z. and Elena P. (2004) studied job satisfaction among school teachers in Cyprus. This research examined job satisfaction and motivation among teachers in Cyprus - a small developing country in the Eastern Mediterranean. An adapted version of the questionnaire developed by the "Teacher 2000 Project" was translated into Greek and used for the purposes of this study that had a sample of 461 teachers and administrators. The findings showed that, unlike other countries in which this questionnaire was used, Cypriot teachers chose this career because of the salary, the hours, and the holidays associated with this profession. The study analyzed how these motives influence the level of satisfaction held by the Cypriot teachers.[7]

Worrell T. G. (2004) conducted a study on school psychologists' job satisfaction: ten years later. This study was designed to replicate nationwide surveys completed in 1982 and 1992. The purpose was to examine and describe the levels of job satisfaction and the relationship between the variables in a national sample of school psychologists belonging to the National Association of School Psychologists (NASP). The sample for this study consisted of 234 respondents who reported being full-time school practitioners. Results indicated that 90% of school psychologists were satisfied or very satisfied with their jobs. The findings showed a gradual increase in overall job satisfaction when compared to the 85.7% in 1982 and the 86% in 1992 who reported being satisfied or very satisfied with their jobs. Participants in the current sample were more satisfied with their job security, independence, and creativity. The only variables demonstrating a significant relationship with job satisfaction were the intent to remain in current position and supervisor certification.[8]

Castillo J. X. and Cano J. (2004) investigated factors explaining job satisfaction among faculty. The purpose of this descriptive-correlational study was to describe the amount of variance in faculty member's overall level of job satisfaction explained by Herzberg, Mausner, and Snyderman's (1959) job motivator and hygiene factors. **A census for this study was conducted among faculty at the College of Food, Agricultural, and Environmental Sciences at the Ohio State University.** The findings of this study were - female faculty members were less satisfied than male faculty member, the factor "work itself" was the most motivating aspect for faculty, the least motivating aspect was "working conditions." The demographic characteristics were negligibly related to overall job satisfaction, all of the job motivator and hygiene factors were moderately or substantially related to overall job satisfaction, the factors "recognition," "supervision," and "relationships" explained the variability among faculty members' overall level of job satisfaction.[9]

Josias B. A. (2005) conducted a study on the relationship between job satisfaction and absenteeism in a selected field services section within an electricity utility in the Western Cape. The aim of the present study was to determine whether there is a relationship between job satisfaction and absenteeism in a selected department within an Electricity Utility in the Western Cape. One hundred and twenty one (121) respondents completed a biographical questionnaire as well as a Job Satisfaction Survey (JSS) to identify their levels of job satisfaction. To ascertain the extent of absenteeism, respondents were asked to report on their number of days absent and their absence frequency within a six month period. The relationship between biographical variables (gender, age, number of dependents, job level, tenure and marital status) and job satisfaction was also investigated. The study found that the six biographical characteristics significantly explained the variance in job satisfaction. The variance accounted for by these six variables was however, relatively small. Job level and tenure were the best predictors of job satisfaction in the selected sample. There was a statistically significant inverse relationship between the frequency of absence, number of days absent and the job satisfaction levels.[10]

Luddy N. (2005) conducted a study on job satisfaction amongst employees at a public health institution in the Western Cape. The primary objective of this study was to ascertain the levels of job satisfaction experienced amongst employees at a public health institution in the Western Cape region. For the purpose of this study a quantitative, non-probability convenience sampling design was used to assess job satisfaction. The sample group (N = 203) consisted of permanent and contract male and female staff members on salary levels 2 to 13, extending across the following occupational classes: Pharmacist, Pharmacist Assistant, Auxiliary Service Officer, Administrative Clerk, Director, Personnel Officer, Administrative Officer, State Accountant and Personnel Practitioner. Results indicated that employees at the public health institution in the Western Cape expressed satisfaction with their co-workers, followed by the nature of the work and the supervision they receive. Opportunities for promotion and pay emerged as major sources of dissatisfaction. With the exception of marital status, the relationship between occupational class, race, gender, educational level, tenure, age, income and job status with job satisfaction was found to be significant. It was recommended that a proportionate stratified random sample should be utilised for future research.[11]

Rama Devi V. (2006) investigated job satisfaction of the teaching staff in the universities. Data were collected from 200 teaching staff - 100 members from University of Hyderabad, a Central University and 100 members from Sri Krishnadevaraya University, a State University. The results showed that teaching staff in the University of Hyderabad were highly satisfied with their jobs when compared to the teaching staff in Sri Krishnadevaraya University. The teaching staff in both the universities was more satisfied with nature of their job dimension and least satisfied with the facilities provided to them. The results also revealed that average job satisfaction score and average score of needs met were significantly related in both the universities.[12]

Gautam M., Mandal K. and Dalal R. S. (2006) conducted a study to measure the level of job satisfaction of the faculty members of Faculty of Veterinary Sciences and Animal Husbandry, Sher-e-Kashmir University of Agricultural Sciences and Technology of Jammu and to explore the variation in the job satisfaction level. The overall job satisfaction of the faculty members was moderate. The younger faculty members were more satisfied as compared to those with a longer service period although the relationship was not linear. There was insignificant difference between those holding masters degree and those who have attained Ph. D.[13]

Siripak S. (2006) investigated job satisfaction of academic staff in Mahidol University. In this study sample included 350 academic staff members employed in Mahidol University. Data analysis was done through t-tests and ANOVA. The results concluded that overall job satisfaction of Mahidol University's academic staffs was at a moderate level. When comparing each type of satisfaction, the results indicated the highest level of job satisfaction was academic satisfaction, followed by cultural support satisfaction, administrative satisfaction, and academic service satisfaction. There was a significant difference between age, marital status, educational level, academic position, income, duration of work, and position and the level of job satisfaction. Gender was the only personal characteristic that indicated no significant difference in overall job satisfaction.[14]

Chimanikire P., Mutandwa E., Gadzirayi C. T., Muzondo N. and Mutandwa B. (2007) investigated the factors affecting job satisfaction among academic professionals in tertiary institutions in Zimbabwe. Total of 80 respondents were selected randomly from departmental lists and interviewed using structured questionnaires. Key informants such as administration personnel were also interviewed using semi-structured schedules. The results of the study showed that a greater proportion of the academic staff was not satisfied with their jobs. Reasons for dissatisfaction include high volume of work, inadequate salaries, allowances, loans to facilities purchase of housing stands and cars.[15]

Rahman M. I. and Parveen R. (2009) investigated the factors contributing to the satisfaction and dissatisfaction of the public and private university teachers of Bangladesh. It was found that there was a significant difference between public and private university teachers regarding job satisfaction on different factors. It also compared the overall job satisfaction level and the nature of satisfaction among the public and private university teachers. The result revealed that teachers' age and job experience do not have any significant influence on job satisfaction though gender disparities were profound among their responses.[16]

Howard T. T. (2009) conducted a study the purpose of which was to investigate the job satisfaction of men and women administrators in higher education in four-year public institutions in Alabama. In conducting the study, the researcher selected four public four-year higher education institutions from a list of 14 four-year public institutions governed by the Alabama Commission on Higher Education. The total number of administrators in the data set was fifty six (56). The administrator demographic variables were as follows: (a) gender, (b) ethnicity, (c) age group, (d) marital status, (e) education level, (f) years of administrator experience, (g) salary, and (h) job title. Results from the statistical analysis showed that in terms of present job duties, pay, opportunities for promotion, and supervision, the administrators who participated in this study were satisfied. The administrators expressed a level of dissatisfaction with the people with whom they work and their job in general. There was no statistically significant difference in overall job satisfaction of the male and female administrators surveyed. There was no statistically significant difference in overall job satisfaction, work climate, and job structure between the male and female administrators who participated in this study. The findings indicated that male administrators were more satisfied with their work climate than the female administrators; however, the findings were still not statistically significant at the 0.05 level.[17]

Amiri M., Khosravi A. A. and Mokhtari A. A. (2010) conducted a study on job satisfaction and its influential factors. In this descriptive study, conducted in 2008, the participants were 384 workers in Shahroud University of Medical Sciences (SUMS) selected through simple random sampling procedure. This study aimed at determining the job satisfaction level of the staff in SUMS, northern Iran, and its influential factors. The mean of the overall satisfaction was 13.02 out of 20. Regarding the facets of job satisfaction, work, coworkers, supervisor, and promotion had the highest means, respectively. Pearson and Spearman correlation coefficients showed a significant relationship between overall satisfaction and the facets (p = 0.001). Analysis of variance also showed significant difference in overall satisfaction based on organizational units; however, no significant relationship was observed between overall satisfaction and gender, degree, age, job experience and type of employment.[18]

Ch'ng H. K., Chong W. K. and Nakesvari (2010) examined the satisfaction level of Penang private college lecturers. This research was mainly undertaken to investigate on the significance of factors such as management support, salary and promotion opportunities in affecting the job satisfaction and further to explore on the moderating effect of age, gender, and length of working on the relationships between management support, salary and promotion opportunities and job satisfaction of private college lecturers in Penang. The result from this research showed that management support, salary and promotion opportunities are significant in determining the job satisfaction. It was also discovered that there is significant effect of length of working in moderating the relationship between management support and job satisfaction of selected private college lecturers in Penang.[19]

Ghazi S. R., Ali R., Shahzada G. and Israr M. (2010) investigated university teachers' job satisfaction in the North West Frontier Province of Pakistan. All the university teachers working in North West Frontier Province of Pakistan constituted the population of this study. A sample of 108 university teachers was drawn from this population. A questionnaire following the theoretical framework of Herzberg's two factor theory was developed. The findings show that university teachers were generally satisfied with their jobs. However teachers were neutral with dimensions: working conditions, organizational policies and practices, recognition, supervision technical and promotion opportunities. The teachers were satisfied with work variety, creativity, moral values, compensation, work itself, colleagues' cooperation, responsibility, ability utilization, authority, activity, social status, job security, achievement and students' interaction.[20]

Olorunsola E. O. (2010) conducted a study on job satisfaction and gender factor of administrative staff in South West Nigeria Universities. The study investigated the level of job satisfaction of male and female administrative staff in South West Nigeria Universities. The research design used was a descriptive survey type. The population consisted of all the senior administrative staff in the universities, out of which a sample of 400 respondents made up of 100 respondents from each of the state and federal universities. The result of the analysis showed that the level of job satisfaction of administrative staff in both federal and state universities was high. It was also revealed that there was no significant difference in the job satisfaction of administrative staff in the universities. It was revealed that there was significant difference in the job satisfaction of male and female administrative staff in the universities.[21]

Ali M. A., Zaman T. U., Tabassum F. and Iqbal Z. (2011) conducted a study the purpose of which was to explore job satisfaction of secondary school teachers working in the secondary schools at district Sahiwal in Pakistan. The sample of 200 secondary school teachers was taken randomly from district Sahiwal for this research study. The response rate was 100%. In order to collect required data for the study, the Minnesota Satisfaction Questionnaire (MSQ) was used as a tool. Mean score of twenty dimensions were calculated and t-test was also applied for the sake of comparison of job satisfaction of male-female and urban-rural teachers. The findings showed that the secondary school teachers were slightly satisfied with the basic eight dimensions (out of twenty) of a job i.e. ability utilization, advancement, education policies, independence, compensation, creativity, recognition and working condition. There was a significant difference of job satisfaction between male and female secondary school teachers. However no significant difference was found between the job satisfaction of urban and rural teachers.[22]

Ghazi S. R., Shahzad S., Shahzada G. and Gillani U. S. (2011) conducted a study on job satisfaction of head teachers for the selected twenty dimensions of job. The population of this study consisted of all head teachers of government elementary schools of district Toba Tek Singh in the Punjab. The teachers of all categories, who were working as head teachers in government elementary schools in district Toba Tek Singh, filled the questionnaires. Due to the devolution of power at district level; to make the results more authentic at district level sample was identical to the population. It was found that Compensation, Working Conditions, Social Status, and School Policies and Practices were the facets of job which contributed to low satisfaction. The head teachers were satisfied with the facets of their job, i.e. Advancement, Social Service, Creativity, Recognition, Supervision Human Relation, Security, Independence, Colleagues, Supervision Technical, Authority, Responsibility, Achievement, Ability Utilization and Variety. The head teachers were found to be "Very Satisfied" with Activity and Moral Values dimensions of their job.[23]

Nadeem M. (2011) conducted a study on job satisfaction factors of faculty members at university of Balochistan. The major purpose of this descriptive-correlational study was to examine factors affecting job satisfaction of faculty members of University of Balochistan which is explained by Herzberg job motivator and hygiene factors. A random sample of 120 faculty member of Balochistan University was selected as a statistical sample. Employing a descriptive-correlative survey method and data were collected through questionnaire. The faculty members were generally satisfied with their jobs. However, male faculty members were less satisfied than female faculty members. The factor "work itself" was the most motivating aspect for faculty. The least motivating aspect was "working conditions." The demographic characteristics were negligibly related to overall job satisfaction. The factors "work itself," and "advancement" explained 60 percent of the variance among faculty members' overall level of job satisfaction. The demographic characteristics (age, years of experience, academic rank, degree) were negligibly related to overall job satisfaction.[24]

Mangi R. A., Soomro H. J., Ghumro I. A., Abidi A. R. and Jalbani A. A. (2011) conducted a study of job satisfaction among non Ph. D. faculty in universities. 125 non Ph. D. faculty members from various universities of Sindh at a response rate of 83% participated in the survey. The 81% data was reliable for the analysis. The majority of the respondents was male, graduate, below 30 years of age, married and had job experience of more than 5 years. The results showed that overall job satisfaction among the non-Ph. D. faculty members of universities was very low. The motivator and job satisfaction components have significant impact on the overall job satisfaction of the non - Ph.D. faculty. Considering the results, the management of the universities was recommended to focus on the job motivators (Advancement, Recognition) hygiene factors (Interpersonal Relationship, Policies, Compensation) of the non - Ph.D. faculty for the improvement of job satisfaction and performance.[25]

Wadhwa Daljeet Singh, Verghese Manoj and Wadhwa Dalvinder Singh (2011) conducted a study on factors influencing employee job satisfaction - a study in cement industry of Chhattisgarh. It was found that all the three factors i.e. behavioral, organizational and environmental factors have a significant impact on employee job satisfaction since the significance level is less than 0.05 i.e. 0.000 for behavioral factors and 0.010 for organizational factors and 0.013 for environmental factors.[26]

Shabbir M. S., Ahmed K., Lawler J. J. and Shahbaz M. (2011) conducted a research to investigate the determinants of teacher satisfaction and to find the level of satisfaction with their job, in terms of various factors such as working conditions, pay and benefits and relationship with co-workers in Pakistani universities. The data were collected by using a questionnaire method. 110 university teachers were surveyed to find the level of satisfaction with their job, in terms of with various factors such as working conditions, pay and benefits and relationship with co-workers. Convenience sampling was used, and a total of 88 usable questionnaires were returned. Findings of the research showed that job satisfaction was highly dependent upon factors like, pay-benefits, relationship with co-workers and working conditions.[27]

Muindi F. K. (2011) examined the relationship between participation in decision making and job satisfaction among academic staff in public University of Nairobi. This study was conducted on the positivism approach to research. The study adopted a descriptive survey research design. The population of the study was all non-management members of academic staff at the School of Business, University of Nairobi. A structured questionnaire was prepared and distributed to all selected respondents. The study comprised of two major variables, namely participation in decision making, which was the independent variable and job satisfaction which was the dependent variable. A five point scale was used to collect data and analysis was based on averages, percentage, correlation coefficient and linear regression. The findings indicated that a significantly strong positive correlation was found between job satisfaction and participation in decision-making (r = 0.888). The findings indicated also a positively strong correlation between participation in decision-making and job satisfaction in relation to general working conditions (r = 0.640), pay and promotion potential (r = 0.703), use of skills and abilities (r = 0.895), job design (r = 0.750) and job feedback (r = 0.632). The findings indicated that the level of job satisfaction for workers at the School of Business increased proportionately with an increase in their level of participation in decision-making.[28]

Swarnalatha C. and Sureshkrishna G. (2012) studied job satisfaction among employees of automotive industries in India. The research was conducted among 234 employees of automotive industries in India and the result of this study showed that the job satisfaction level of employees was medium and the top management leadership needed to take attention of enhancing the employee job satisfaction level. The result also shows that there was a significant relationship was approved between 1) employee empowerment, 2) teamwork, 3) employee compensation and 4) management leadership.[29]

Strydom L., Nortje N., Beukes R., Esterhuyse K. and Westhuizen J. (2012) examined the job satisfaction amongst teachers at special needs schools. The research group consisted of

101 teachers working at six different special schools situated in various parts of the Bloemfontein area, two in the Mangaung area, and four were situated in suburban areas. The group consisted of English- and Afrikaans-speaking teachers of both genders and from different race groups. The data for this study were compiled by means of a short biographical questionnaire and the Minnesota Satisfaction Questionnaire. The results indicated that the teachers experienced an average level of job satisfaction. In addition to this finding, differences were also found in the levels of job satisfaction between different races, but not between genders.[30]

SivaKumar M. and Siddique A. M. (2012) conducted a study on job satisfaction for it professionals in Chennai city. The sampling population of this research included 216 software professionals of IT industries in Chennai. The results have shown that IT professionals were very much dissatisfied with fringe benefits, nature of work and contingent rewards while moderately satisfied with Pay, promotion and supervision factors.[31]

Salehi M., Gahderi A. and Rostami V. (2012) conducted a study of job satisfaction between external and internal auditors: an Iranian scenario. Results of this research revealed that internal auditors had lower authority than external auditors. Further, internal auditors had low level satisfaction from supervisors than external auditors in Iran.[32]

Munshi N. M. (2012) did a comparative analysis of job satisfaction level of management teachers of MBA colleges in

Gujarat State. The sample population comprised of 172 management teachers (40% of the population) working in different MBA colleges of Gujarat. All the institutes were approved by AICTE, New Delhi. The sample MBA institutes had intake capacity of varying size ranging from 30 students to 120 students across the state. Out of 172 MBA teachers, 108 (62.8%) were working as lectures, 45 (26.2%) were employed as Assistant Professors, 7 (4.1%) were employed as Professors and 12 (7.0%) were employed as Principals/Directors in different institutions. All the teachers were full time employees in their respective management colleges. This study revealed that there was no systematic association between salary paid by the management colleges, length of service and the degree of job satisfaction of management teachers of Gujarat, whereas there was systematic association between total years of experience, age, intake capacity of students and the degree of job satisfaction of management teachers of Gujarat.[33]

REFERENCES

1) Bronski D. C. and Cook S. (1994). The job satisfaction of allied health professionals. Journal of Allied Health, Vol. 7, pp. 281-287.

2) Okerlund V. W., Jacson P. B. and Parsons R. J. (1994). Factors affecting recruitment of physical therapy personnel in Utah. Physical Therapy, Vol. 74(2), pp. 177-184.

3) Speakman C. B., Pleasant J. M. and Sutton G. B. (1996). The job satisfaction of physical therapists. Physiotherapy Research International, Vol. 1(4), pp. 247-254.

4) Khan M. A. (1999). A comparative study of job satisfaction among teachers of government and private secondary schools in Karachi. A Ph.D. thesis, Hamdard University, Karachi.

5) Brewer E. W. and Landers J. M. (2003). Job satisfaction among industrial and technical teacher educators. Journal of Industrial Teacher Education, Vol. 40 (2), retrieved from http://scholar.lib.vt.edu/ejournals/JITE/v40n on 6th July 2013.

6) Murray R. A. (1999). Job satisfaction of professional and paraprofessional library staff at the University Of North Carolina at Chapel Hill. A Master's paper for the M.S. in Library Science Degree, University of North Carolina, Chapel Hill.

7) Michalinos Z. and Elena P. (2004). Job satisfaction among school teachers in Cyprus. Journal of Educational Administration, Volume 42 (3), pp. 357-374.

8) Worrell T. G. (2004). School psychologists' job satisfaction: ten years later. A Ph. D. thesis, Virginia Polytechnic Institute and State University, Virginia.

9) Castillo J. X. and Cano J. (2004) investigated factors explaining job satisfaction among faculty. Journal of Agricultural Education, Vol. 45 (3), pp. 65-74.

10) Josias B. A. (2005). The relationship between job satisfaction and absenteeism in a selected field services section within an electricity utility in the Western Cape. A mini-thesis for the degree of Master of Commerce, University of the Western Cape.

11) Luddy N. (2005). Study on job satisfaction amongst employees at a public health institution in the Western Cape. A mini-thesis for the degree of Magister Commercii, University of the Western Cape.

12) Rama Devi V. (2006). Job satisfaction among university teachers. SCMS Journal of Indian Management, Vol.3 (4), pp. 87-94.

13) Gautam M., Mandal K. and Dalal R. S. (2006). Job satisfaction of faculty members of veterinary sciences: An analysis. Livestock Research for Rural Development.

14) Siripak S. (2006). Job satisfaction of academic staff in Mahidol University. A thesis for M. Ed., Mahidol University.

15) Chimanikire P., Mutandwa E., Gadzirayi C. T., Muzondo N. and Mutandwa B. (2007) investigated the factors affecting job satisfaction among academic professionals in tertiary

institutions in Zimbabwe. African Journal of Business Management, African Journal of Business Management, Vol. 1(6), pp. 166-175.

16) Rahman M. I. and Parveen R. (2009). Job Satisfaction: A study among public and private university teachers of Bangladesh. Retrieved from http://ssrn.com/abstract=1155303 on 15th November 2012.

17) Howard T. T. (2009). Administrator job satisfaction in higher education. A Ph. D. thesis, Auburn University, Alabama.

18) Amiri M., Khosravi A. A. and Mokhtari A. A. (2010) conducted a study on job satisfaction and its influential factors. Journal of Research in Health Sciences, Vol. 10 (1), pp. 42-46.

19) Ch'ng H. K., Chong W. K. and Nakesvari (2010). The satisfaction level of Penang private college lecturers. International Journal of Trade, Economics and Finance, Vol. 1 (2), pp. 168-172.

20) Ghazi S. R., Ali R., Shahzada G. and Israr M. (2010). University teachers' job satisfaction in the North West Frontier Province of Pakistan. Asian Social Science, Vol. 6 (11), pp. 188-192.

21) Olorunsola E. O. (2010). Job satisfaction and gender factor of administrative staff in South West Nigeria Universities. EABR and ETLC Conference Proceedings, Dublin, Ireland, pp. 91-95.

22) Ali M. A., Zaman T. U., Tabassum F. and Iqbal Z. (2011). A study of job satisfaction of secondary school teachers. Journal of Education and Practice, Vol. 2 (1), pp. 32-37.

23) Ghazi S. R., Shahzad S., Shahzada G. and Gillani U. S. (2011). Study on job satisfaction of head teachers for the selected twenty dimensions of job. International Journal of Academic Research, Vol. 3(1), pp. 651-654.

24) Nadeem M. (2011). Study on job satisfaction factors of faculty members at university of Balochistan. International Journal of Academic Research, Vol. 3(1), pp. 267-272.

25) Mangi R. A., Soomro H. J., Ghumro I. A., Abidi A. R. and Jalbani A. A. (2011). A study of job satisfaction among non Ph. D. faculty in universities. Australian Journal of Business and Management Research, Vol.1 (7), pp. 83-90.

26) Wadhwa Daljeet Singh, Verghese Manoj and Wadhwa Dalvinder Singh (2011). Factors influencing employee job satisfaction - a study in cement industry of Chhattisgarh. International Journal of Management and Business Studies, Vol. 1 (3), pp. 109-111.

27) Shabbir M. S., Ahmed K., Lawler J. J. and Shahbaz M. (2011). Affect of working environment on job satisfaction in Pakistan. World Review of Entrepreneurship, Management and Sustainable Development, Vol. 7 (1), pp.52–61.

28) Muindi F. K. (2011). The relationship between participation in decision making and job satisfaction among academic staff

in the School of Business, University of Nairobi. Journal of Human Resources Management Research, pp. 1-34.

29) Swarnalatha C. and Sureshkrishna G. (2012). Job satisfaction among employees of automotive industries in India. International Journal of Future Computer and Communication, Vol. 1 (3), pp. 245-248.

30) Strydom L., Nortje N., Beukes R., Esterhuyse K. and Westhuizen J. (2012). Job satisfaction amongst teachers at special needs schools. South African Journal of Education, Vol. 32, pp. 255-266.

31) SivaKumar M. and Siddique A. M. (2012). Job satisfaction for it professionals in Chennai city. IJEMR, Vol. 2 (3), pp. 1-8.

32) Salehi M., Gahderi A. and Rostami V. (2012). Job satisfaction between external and internal auditors: an Iranian scenario. Research Journal of Applied Sciences, Engineering and Technology, Vol. 4(10), pp. 1300 -1309.

33) Munshi N. M. (2012). A comparative analysis of job satisfaction level of management teachers of MBA colleges in Gujarat State. A Ph. D. thesis, Saurashtra University, Rajkot.

CHAPTER – III

RESEARCHES RELATING TO THE JOB INVOLVEMENT

Mitchell V. F., Vishwanath B. and Timothy E. (1975) investigated the relationship between job involvement (JI) and central life interest (CLI) for a sample of automobile workers chosen from three organizational levels containing unskilled employees, skilled workmen and foremen. Possible associations of job involvement and work as the "Central Life Interest" with job levels in the occupational hierarchy, age of the individuals and the length of employment were also explored. The results disconfirmed the hypothesized positive relationship between job involvement (JI) and central life interest (CLI). In fact a low but significant négative relationship was obtained between job involvement (JI) and central life interest (CLI). Job levels, age and length of employment were found to hâve negligible influence on both job involvement (JI) and central life interest (CLI).[1]

Lious and Bazemore (1994) conducted a study on the job involvement of social workers. They administered a research on professional orientation and job involvement among juvenile detention caseworkers. An anonymous questionnaire was distributed to 109 detention caseworkers of two regional metropolitan detention centers in two cities in a southeastern state of the United States. The total response rate was 63%. Job involvement was the dependent variable in the study whereas professional orientation and personal and job characteristics (i.e. age, sex education, tenure, and perceived job security) were used as independent variables. Regression analysis showed that job security in the study was the major determinant of job involvement among the detention caseworkers. The study results also supported the argument that job involvement is influenced more by job-related factors than personal characteristics.[2]

Aminabhavi V. A. (1996) found in his study that the professionals with high job involvement have significantly higher quality of life in comparison to the low job involvement.[3]

Venakatachalam J. and Reddy K. S. (1996) conducted a study to find out the impact of job level, Job tenure and type of organization on job involvement and job satisfaction among employees working in three organizations viz., banks, schools and government offices. The data obtained on these scale were analyzed by means of analysis of variance. The results showed that there was significant influence of job level on work involvement and job involvement, but it did not significantly influenced job satisfaction. The type of organizations in which the employees were working significantly influenced the job satisfaction but not work and job involvement. The result further revealed that the job tenure did not show significant impact on job involvement, work involvement and job satisfaction.[4]

Aminabhavi V.A. and Dharanendraih A.S. (1997) conducted a study to identify the factors that contribute to job involvement among doctors, engineers, lawyers and teachers. The age group of the subjects varied between 30-60 years. Results showed that the selection of occupation expressed with regard to job satisfaction and socio- cultural background that contributed significantly job involvement of the professionals. The results was interpreted that the professional who choose their occupation and expressed higher job satisfaction and the professional who came from upper middle stratum of socio- cultural background showed higher job involvement than their counter parts.[5]

Jaswant V. and Naveen K. (1997) conducted a study to examine the interactive effects of age, gender and type – A behavior pattern on job stress and job involvement of bank employees. The results indicated that gender and type-A behavior significantly influenced job involvement of bank employees. The results also showed significant interaction effect of age, gender and type –A behavior pattern on job stress.[6]

Venakatachalam J., Reddy K. S. and Samullah S. (1998) carried out study on the employees working in banks, schools and government offices. The study was aimed to find out the effect of job level, organizational identity on job involvement and job satisfaction. The results showed that supervisors were more job involved and more satisfied with their job in comparison to their subordinates. Results also revealed that the employees working in banks were more job involved and showed greater level of job satisfaction than those working in schools and government offices. It was also found that job level had significant effect on job involvement and job satisfaction and the organizational identity significantly influenced job satisfaction but not the job involvement.[7]

Biswas U. N. (1998) studied the influence of life style stressors- performance, frustration, threat and physical damage on organizational commitment and job involvement of managers, supervisors and workers of large and medium public and private sector organization. The respondents were asked to complete the demographical information schedule, life style stressors questionnaire, job involvement questionnaire and the perceived organizational questionnaire. The results revealed that the performance, threat and frustration emerged significant predictors of organizational commitment. Whereas none of the stressors emerged as predictor of job involvement the result also indicated that managers scored high on job involvement as compared to the supervisors and workers. The workers showed greater performance stress.[8]

Joshi G. (1998) compared the job satisfaction, job involvement and work involvement among the employees of private and public sectors. Result indicated that the public and private sector employees differ significantly in term of their job satisfaction, job involvement and work involvement.[9]

Naaz H. (1999) studied the job involvement of textile mill workers in relation to job characteristics and demographic variables. The result also indicated that the task identity and skills variety were found predictors of job involvement.[10]

Patel M. K. (1999) conducted a study to find out the influence of age, organizational commitment on job involvement of nationalized and co-operative bank employees. The sample consisted of 200 employees (100 in each group). Mowday's organizational commitment scale was administered on the sample. The result revealed that the younger employees both nationalized and co-operative bank employees differ significantly with their middle age group employees. The younger employees were found less job involved and showed less organizational commitment than the employees of middle age group. The employees from nationalized bank showed higher commitment then those of the employees of co-operative bank.[11]

Srivastava S. K. (2001) conducted a study to examine job involvement and mental health among 60 executives and 15 supervisors with work experience ranging from 8 to 30 years. Result revealed that executives felt more involved in the job than the supervisor. There was a significant association between job involvement and mental health.[12]

Ahmad A. and Ansari S. A. (2002) conducted a study on craftsman from various small scale industries and noted that job involvement was influenced by the interaction between income and job tenure. [13]

Allam Z. (2002) examined job involvement of bank employees in relation to job anxiety, personality characteristics, job burnout, age and gender. The result revealed that the job anxiety, job burnout, age and gender were significantly related to job involvement. [14]

Mishra A. K. and Wagh A. (2004) conducted a study on job involvement dimension between public and private sector executives. Two groups of executives differed significantly on mean score. Further they pointed out that reward, work culture and environment, challenging job, delegation of authority and responsibility were found to be potential factors for job involvement. [15]

Mishra P. C. and Minum S. (2005) made an attempt to find out the relationship of social support and job involvement in prison officers. Job Involvement Scale developed by Kapoor and Singh and Social Support Scale developed by Cohen et al., were administered on a sample of 200 prison officers incidentally selected from different jails in U.P. and Sampoornanand Jail Training Institute, Lucknow (U.P.). The result shows that social support (overall) and its dimensions, namely, appraisal support, tangible support and belonging support have significant positive relationship with job involvement. Stepwise Multiple Regression Analysis suggests that overall social support is a significant predictor of job involvement in prison officers. The other predictors are belonging, support, appraisal support and tangible support.[16]

Liao C. and Lee C. (2009) conducted an empirical study of employee job involvement and personality traits: the case of Taiwan. The research population consisted of small and medium-sized enterprises (SMEs) in the plastics industry in Taiwan. Using questionnaire data gathered from 272 Taiwanese plastics industry employees. The study tested five hypotheses using structural equations. Empirical findings showed that neuroticism related negatively to employee job involvement, whereas extroversion, openness, agreeableness, and conscientiousness related positively to it.[17]

Govender S. and Parumasur S. B. (2010) assessed the level of and relationship between employee motivation and job involvement among permanent and temporary employees in various departments in a financial institution. This cross-sectional study was undertaken on 145 employees who were drawn from various departments (acquisitions, automated, client operations, collections, corporate, motor, other) at a branch of a financial institution by using a simple random sampling technique. Data were collected using the Employee Motivation Questionnaire (Fourie, 1989) and the Job Involvement Questionnaire (Lodahl and Kejner, 1965) and was analyzed using descriptive and inferential statistics. They found that there were significant intercorrelations among the majority of dimensions of employee motivation (economic rewards, intrinsic satisfaction, social relationships) and sub-dimensions of job involvement (response to work, expression of being job-involved, sense of duty towards work, feelings of guilt regarding unfinished work and absenteeism).[18]

Mohsan F., Nawaz M. M., Khan M. S., Shaukat Z., Islam T., Aslam N., Arslan H. M., Chouhan M. Q. and Niazi M. K. (2011) attempted to examine the impact of job involvement on organizational citizenship behavior (OCB) and in-role job performance of employees working in banking sector of Pakistan. The data were collected from 112 subjects using the questionnaire forms and then Microsoft Excel and SPSS 16 was used for data analysis. The findings of the study revealed that job involvement was positively correlated with both organizational citizenship behavior (OCB) and in-role job performance but the relative impact of job involvement on OCB was stronger than on in-role job performance.[19]

Abutayeh B. and Al-Qatawneh M. (2012) conducted a research which aimed to examine the effect of Human Resource Practices on job involvement in an Arabic country namely; Jordan. Six of the major Human Resource Practices are included in this research, namely: job analysis, selection, training, performance appraisal, compensation and career management. We administered surveys to 15 companies in Jordan and acquired a sample of 272 valid cases. Results show that all Human Resource Practices have a positive effect on job involvement. When considering job involvement, selection exhibits the highest effect whereas training has the lowest effect.[20]

REFERENCES

1) Mitchell V. F., Vishwanath B. and Timothy E. (1975). On the relationship between job involvement and central life interest. Industrial Relations, Vol. 30 (2), pp. 166-180.

2) Lious K. T. and Bazemore G. B. (1994). Professional orientation and job involvement among detention caseworkers. Public Administration Quarterly, Summer, pp. 223-236.

3) Aminabhavi V. A. (1996). Quality of life of professionals in relation to their job involvement and socio-cultural background. Paper presented in 1st Asian and 32nd Annual Conference of IAAP at Aligarh.

4) Venakatachalam J. and Reddy K. S. (1996). Impact of job level and job tenure on work involvement, job involvement and job satisfaction in different organizations. Human Relations. pp. 76-81.

5) Aminabhavi V. A. and Dharanendraih A. S. (1997). A study of the factor contributing to job involvement of professional. Indian Journal of Psychometry and Education, Vol. 28(2), pp. 109-112.

6) Jaswant V. and Naveen K. (1997). Job stress and job involvement among bank employees. Indian Journal of Applied Psychology, Vol. 34(2), pp. 33-38.

7) Venakatachalam J., Reddy K. S. and Samullah S. (1998). Effect of job level and organizational identity on job involvement and job satisfaction: A study of different

organizations. Management and Labour Studies, Vol. 23(3), pp. 421-427.

8) Biswas U. N. (1998). Life style stressors, organizational commitments, job involvement and perceived organizational effectiveness across job levels. Indian Journal of Industrial Relations, Vol. 34(1), pp. 55-72.

9) Joshi G. (1998). Job satisfaction, job involvement and work involvement among the employees of private and public sectors. Psychological Studies, Vol. 43(3), pp. 85-90.

10) Naaz H. (1999). Job characteristics and demographic variables predictor of job involvement of textile mill workers. Journal of Indian Academy of Applied Psychology, Vol. 25(1), pp. 75-78.

11) Patel M. K. (1999). A study of impact of age on job involvement and organizational commitment of Nationalized and Co-operative bank employees. Journal of Indian Academy of Applied Psychology, Vol. 25(1), pp. 65-70.

12) Srivastava S. K. (2001). Job involvement and mental health among executive and supervisors. Journal of Community Guidance, Vol. 18(3), pp. 365-372.

13) Ahmad A. and Ansari S. A. (2002). Effect of income and job tenure on job involvement. A study of Craftsman. Journal of Community Guidance and Research. Vol. 17(3), pp. 271-275.

14) Allam Z. (2002). A study of job involvement among bank employees related to job anxiety, personality characteristics

and job burnout. Unpublished doctoral thesis, Department of Psychology, Aligarh Muslim University, Aligarh.

15) Mishra A. K. and Wagh A. (2004). A comparative study of job involvement among business executives. Indian Journal of Training and Development. Vol. 34(2), pp. 79-84.

16) Mishra P. C. and Minum S. (2005). Social support and job involvement in prison officers. Journal of the Indian Academy of Applied Psychology, Vol. 31 (1-2), pp. 7-11.

17) Liao C. and Lee C. (2009). An empirical study of employee job involvement and personality traits: the case of Taiwan. International Journal of Economics and Management, Vol. 3(1), pp. 22-36.

18) Govender S. and Parumasur S. B. (2010). The relationship between employee motivation and job involvement. SAJEMS, Vol. 13 (3), pp. 237-253.

19) Mohsan F., Nawaz M. M., Khan M. S., Shaukat Z., Islam T., Aslam N., Arslan H. M., Chouhan M. Q. and Niazi M. K. (2011). Impact of job involvement on organizational citizenship behavior (OCB) and in-role job performance: A study on banking sector of Pakistan. European Journal of Social Sciences, Vol. 24 (4), pp.494-502.

20) Abutayeh B. and Al-Qatawneh M. (2012). The effect of human resource management practices on job involvement in selected private companies in Jordan. Canadian Social Science Vol. 8 (2), pp. 50-57.

CHAPTER – IV
RESEARCHES RELATING TO THE ORGANIZATIONAL COMMITMENT

Sheldon (1971) found out that organizational commitment increases with the number of years spent in an organization. This is because length of service suggests the accumulation of organizational career; it binds one to the organization, for example in pension or profit sharing plans.[1]

Alluto, Hrebiniak, and Alonso (1973) conducted a study in which they discovered a curvilinear relationship between age and employee organizational commitment. In this study, usable data were obtained from 318 elementary and secondary school teachers and from 395 professional nurses. Mean levels of employee commitment by age categories were: 26 years or less - 10.68, ages 27 years to 44 years - 10.53 and ages 45 years and up - 10.94.[2]

Shoemaker, Snizek, and Bryant (1977) conducted an organizational tenure study that involved federal and state forest rangers. Positive correlations between organizational commitment and organizational tenure were obtained for both federal and state forest rangers. Federal rangers (n = 62) yielded a correlation of 0.22. The correlation between organizational commitment and organizational tenure for state rangers (n = 58) was 0.17.[3]

Wiener and Vardi (1980) looked at the effect that organizational commitment had on commitment to the job and career commitment. Their participants included 56 insurance agents and 85 staff professionals. The researchers reported positive relationships between organizational commitment and the two other types of commitment.[4]

Amernic J. H. and Aranya N. (1983) conducted a study on organizational commitment: testing two theories. It was found that occupational settings as well as organizational level were found to be significant factors of organizational commitment, satisfaction with job scope was found the most powerful predictor of organization commitment and professional commitment was found to be a significant positive predictor of organizational commitment.[5]

Aranya, Kushmir, and Valency (1986) collected data from a sample of 1,040 Canadian Charter Accountants (equivalent of American Certified Public Accountants) and Certified Public Accountants from the California Society of Certified Public Accountants. The sample consisted of 1,000 men and 40 women; the purpose of the research was to test the commitment level of women in a male-dominated profession. The female accountants in this study demonstrated less organizational commitment than male accountants.[6]

DeCotiis and Summers (1987) undertook a study of 367 managers and their employees. The researchers examined the relationship between organizational commitment and the outcome measures of individual motivation, desire to leave, turnover, and job performance. Organizational commitment was found to be a strong predicator for each of these outcome areas.[7]

Morrow and McElroy (1987) conducted a study in which he reported differences in the levels of organizational commitment based on career stages that were defined by employee age ranges. The sample for this study consisted of 2,200 employees (78% male) from a midwestern department of transportation. The sample was comprised of a variety of employee groups including: administrators, technical and professional employees, clerical and office workers, and service workers. The average age of persons in the sample was 42.7 years. In this study, employees were categorized by age as follows: trial employment period, ages 30 and under; stabilization employment period, ages 31-44 and maintenance employment period, ages 45 and above. Trial period employees obtained a mean organizational commitment rating of 4.13 (SD = 1.01), stabilization period employees obtained a mean rating of 4.31 (SD = 1.03), and maintenance level employees obtained a mean rating of 4.76 (SD = 0.92). Seven-point Likert scales were used to measure commitment in the study. The F ratio was 73.33 and this was significant at the 0.01 level.[8]

Angle and Perry (1991) undertook a study to determine the effect that organizational commitment had on turnover. The participants included 1,244 bus drivers. Findings revealed a negative relationship between turnover and organizational commitment. In short, employees who intended to leave the job were not committed to the organization.[9]

Dunham, Grube, and Castaneda (1994) examined how participatory management and supervisory feedback influenced employee levels of affective, continuance, and normative commitment. The researchers found that when supervisors provided feedback about performance and allowed employees to participate in decision-making, employee levels of affective commitment was stronger than both continuance and normative. That is, employees indicated staying with the organization was more related to wanting to, rather than needing to or feeling they ought to.[10]

Cohen and Kirchmeyer (1995) undertook a study to investigate the relationship between affective, continuance, and normative commitment and the non-work measure of resource enrichment. Their participants included 227 nurses from two hospitals. The researchers found positive relationships between resource enrichment and both affective and normative commitment. However, the relationship between continuance commitment and resource enrichment was negative.[11]

Hawkins W. D. (1997) investigated predictors of affective organizational commitment among high school principals. This study was an assessment of the importance of age, gender, organizational tenure, perceived organizational support, perceived fairness, and perceived autonomy in explaining affective organizational commitment among high school principals in the United States. Stepwise multiple regression was used to determine which independent variables explained a portion of the dependent variable, affective organizational commitment. A sample of 396 high school principals, stratified by gender, was drawn from a national data base developed by Quality Education Data of Denver, CO. The sample consisted of 132 females and 264 males. Data were collected from responses to a questionnaire that was mailed to all persons in the sample. Usable responses were received from 60 females and from 142 males. Results of the stepwise multiple regression indicated that 58 percent of the variation in affective organizational commitment among high school principals was explained by perceived fairness, organizational tenure, perceived organizational support, and high school principals' age. Perceived fairness explained the greatest percentage of variation; age, which entered the regression equation last, explained the least amount of variation. This study indicates that high school principals, first and foremost, valued fairness from school districts in return for their commitment to school districts. The challenge for superintendents and others who work with high school principals is to maintain fairness in educational settings where there are many diverse and competing student needs in the same school district.[12]

Saeed A. (1998) conducted a study to determine the degree of organizational commitment of teachers in government, K. M. C.

and private primary schools of Karachi. The population of the study consisted of approximately 25,000 teachers of Karachi. Stratified random sampling was used. The total sample size consisted of 240 teachers drawn from 52 schools. It was concluded that i) the government school teachers were significantly less committed than their counterparts in K. M. C. and private schools, ii) the female teachers were more committed than the male teachers, iii) the never married teachers were more committed than the married teachers, iv) the less experienced teachers were more committed than the more experienced teachers and v) the less qualified teachers were more committed than the more qualified teachers. No significant differences were found between the younger and older teachers and between the English medium and Urdu medium teachers in respect of their commitment to schools.[13]

Dawley D. D., Stephens R. D. and Stephens D. B. (2005) explored the multi-dimensionality of organizational commitment of volunteer chamber of commerce board members using the Meyer and Allen (1997) organizational commitment scale. The effect of organizational commitment on desirable board members roles was also tested. The result of their study indicated that normative, affective, and continuance commitment based on low alternatives were the three distinct constructs applicable to volunteer employees, and that these components also had a positive effect on board member's role.[14]

Popoola (2007) conducted a study on how work place, biographical, and motivational factors affect the organizational commitment of records officers in federal universities in Nigeria. The study revealed that there were significant differences in the organizational commitment of record officers in the federal universities in Nigeria based on their marital status, work motivation, and job tenure. However, there were no significant differences in the organizational commitment of records officers based on their places of work and religious beliefs.[15]

Nyengane M. H. (2007) investigated the relationship between leadership styles and different types of organizational commitment in Eskom Eastern Region. Information was gathered, using two instruments, from a sample of 86 leaders and 334 raters. The Multifactor Leadership Questionnaire, which was formulated from Bass and Avolio's (1997) Full Range Leadership Development Theory, was used to determine leadership style within the organisation. Employee commitment was captured using Bagraim's (2004) Organizational Commitment, a South African adaptation of Meyer and Allen's (1997) Three-Component Model of employee commitment. Leadership was identified as the independent variable and organizational commitment as the dependent variable. Two-tailed correlation analysis showed that although the relationship was not strong, there was a positive relationship between the transformational leadership behaviours and commitment (affective commitment, continuance commitment and normative commitment). Overall findings from this study suggested that transformational and transactional leadership behaviours do play important roles in determining levels of affective commitment, continuance commitment and normative commitment. These findings also revealed that the laissez-faire leadership behaviour had a negative relationship with affective commitment.[16]

Donya A. L. (2007) conducted a study on organizational commitment of senior woman administrators. The purpose of this study was to examine Senior Woman Administrators (SWAs) perception of organizational commitment. Three types of organizational commitment were surveyed: affective, normative, and continuance commitment. This study was delimited to Senior Woman Administrators (n=66) at National Collegiate Athletic Association (NCAA) Division IAA member institutions across the country. This study used the Organizational Commitment Scale(s) to examine Senior Woman Administrators (SWAs) perceptions of organizational commitment. The study examined the relationship between the demographic variables of ethnicity, marital status, current annual salary, age, years in present position, highest degree earned, and alumni status and organizational commitment. The study also examined the significant differences between the demographic variables and organizational commitment. The results of this study revealed the demographic variables of current annual salary, age, and alumni status were significantly related to affective organizational commitment, ethnicity was significantly related to normative organizational commitment and alumni status was significantly related to continuance organizational commitment. The results also revealed that there were significant differences in mean scores for SWAs perception of affective organizational commitment according to age and alumni status and there was a significant difference in mean scores for SWAs perception of normative organizational commitment according to alumni status.[17]

Khurshid F. (2008) conducted a study to explore personality's big five factors i.e. Extraversion, Agreeableness, Conscientiousness, Neuroticism and Openness and their relationship with occupational role stress and organizational commitment among the public and private sector university teachers. The sample was consisted of 500 university teachers, 250 from public and 250 from private sector universities. Research findings revealed that Neuroticism and Conscientiousness were positively correlated with stress and negatively correlated with commitment. Extraversion, Agreeableness and Openness were negatively correlated with stress and positively correlated with commitment. Teachers with less income and public sector teachers experienced higher stress and low commitment. The older teachers were more committed than younger ones. A significant negative correlation was found between stress and commitment.[18]

Kim M., Jones P. and Rodriguez A. (2008) compared organizational commitment and sport identity among four different work statuses (volunteers, practicum/internship workers, part-time workers, and full-time workers) in a university athletic department. Full-time and practicum/internship workers indicated significantly ($p < 0.05$) higher sport identification than volunteers and part-time workers. Volunteers and practicum/internship workers reported significantly higher affective and normative commitments than part-time employees and significantly lower affective commitment than full-time employees. Thus, it was recommended that athletic departments hire part-time workers cautiously and alternatively consider the potential increased use of practicum/internship workers and volunteers.[19]

Salami S. O. (2008) investigated the relationships of demographic factors (age, marital status, gender, job tenure, and educational level), emotional intelligence, work-role salience, achievement motivation and job satisfaction to organizational commitment of industrial workers. Participants were 320 employees (male = 170, female = 150) randomly selected from 5 service and 5 manufacturing organizations in Oyo State, Nigeria. Measures of biographical data, emotional intelligence, work-role salience, achievement motivation, job satisfaction and organizational commitment were administered on the sample. Hierarchical multiple regression analysis was used to analyse the data collected. Results showed that emotional intelligence, work-role salience, achievement motivation, job satisfaction and all demographic factors except gender significantly predicted organizational commitment of the workers. Findings suggest the need for organizational managements and psychologists to consider the factors investigated when designing programmes for increasing the organizational commitment of the workers.[20]

Butt Z. U. (2009) conducted a research the purpose of which was to extend the existing body of knowledge on the relationship between occupational stress and employees' organizational commitment into the context of non-governmental organizations of Pakistan. The sample of thirty-seven NGOs whose head offices were based in the eight major cities of Pakistan were selected. A sample of 500 NGO employees was randomly collected from the selected NGOs. It was a descriptive correlational study in which scientific methodology was used to answer the research questions. Based upon the review of the recent literature available on the subject, a conceptual framework was developed to study the relationship between occupational stress and organizational commitment in the NGO sector in Pakistan. An inverse relationship was found between occupational stress and organizational commitment. The level of occupational stress experienced by NGO employees was found to be high. The occupational roles that employees play were reported as the main source of stress. The level of employees' organizational commitment was generally moderate but with a tendency towards high. Normative commitment was reported as the strongest form of commitment. Demographic variables of age, experience, job position and income as well as gender significantly influenced the relationship between occupational stress and organizational commitment.[21]

WeiBo Z., Kaur S. and Jun W. (2010) reviewed the characteristics of main approaches to Organizational Commitment from the beginning of conception of Commitment in Becker (1960) till 2009, provided an overview of different eras and domains. Then discussed some new development of Organizational Commitment in commitment tendency or combined influence to organizational outcomes.[22]

Khan M. R., Ziauddin, Jam F. A. and Ramay M. I. (2010) investigated the impact of Organizational Commitment on employee job performance from a sample of 153 public and private and public sector employees of oil and gas sector in Pakistan. The results revealed a positive relationship between organizational commitment and employees' job performance. In the comparative analysis of three dimensions of organizational commitment, normative commitment had a positive and significant impact on employees' job performance. Furthermore, the study explored the employees job performance with four demographic variables, resulting that male employees were high performer vis-à-vis their female counterparts.[23]

Baksh A. M. (2010) conducted a study on organizational commitment of managerial employees: a unified theory and antecedents. The results of this study confirmed that organizational commitment is a multi-dimensional theory with three major domains-affective, continuance, and moral commitment, each of which has a distinct conceptual foundation. The study also confirmed that: (a) affective commitment is based predominantly on psychological factors (b) moral commitment is founded on philosophical, ethical and sociological factors and (c) continuance commitment which is socio-economic by nature focuses predominantly on risk, economic losses, economic gains and labor market conditions that indicate the availability/non-availability of suitable alternative employment.[24]

Anvari R., Amin S. M., Ahmad U. N., Seliman S., and Garmsari M. (2011) investigated the relationships among strategic compensation practices, psychological contract, and affective organizational commitment. In addition, the study aimed to test the mediating effect of psychological contract in the relationship between strategic compensation practices and affective organizational commitment. The study sample comprised 301 non academic staff in the universities of medical sciences in Iran. Results revealed that strategic compensation practices led to perceived fulfillment of psychological contract and the latter, in turn, led to higher affective organizational commitment. In addition, employees with higher levels of affective organizational commitment who perceived a fulfillment of psychological contract were less likely to leave an organization. There was significant relationship between employees' psychological contract and their affective organizational commitment.[25]

Bashir M., Jianqiao L., Zhang Y., Ghazanfar F., Abrar M. and Khan M. M. (2011) evaluated the relationship between high performance work system and organization commitment and the level of organizational commitment among gender (male and female), nature of tenure (regular and contract employees) and job experience. Results based on academic faculty sample of 616 from 22 public sector universities of Pakistan showed that high performance work system was positively and significantly associated with organizational commitment. Kruskal-Wallis test revealed that there was no significant difference in organizational commitment of male and female academic faculty. Academic faculty with regular tenure was more committed than academic faculty with contract tenure. High experience academic faculty was more committed than less experience academic faculty. The results also indicated that gender moderate the relationship between high performance work system and organizational commitment. However moderate effect of tenure and experience were not confirmed.[26]

Akinbode G. A. and Fagbohungbe O. B. (2012) examined the relationship between leadership-behaviour and organizational factors as predictors of workers organizational commitment. A total number of 504 workers selected from private and public sector organizations located in Lagos and Abuja in Nigeria participated in the study. Results revealed a positive progression in the influence of organizational factor on organizational commitment variables. Specifically, junior workers reported more commitment compared to senior management level workers for at least 1.03 times. Result indicated that interpersonal relations and emancipator leadership behaviour had significant positive correlations with organizational commitment variables (job identification, job involvement and job loyalty). Interpersonal relations contributed about 19.3% of the observed variance in workers organizational commitment. Emancipatory leadership-behaviour contributed 10.2% workers organizational commitment, while autocratic/control contributed only 7.1% of the observed variance. Also, productive and patriotic leadership-behaviour did not predict workers organizational commitment, the finding underscores the emergence of various sharp practices in the Nigerian organization in recent times. Perceived leadership behaviours accounted for about 11.6% of the observed variance in organizational commitment.[27]

Islam T., Ahmad Z., Ahmed I., Ahmad A., Saeed M. and Muhammad S. K. (2012) conducted a study to find the influence of compensation and demographical impact on the commitment and job satisfaction of the teachers. Population of the study included all the faculty members of the University of the Punjab, Lahore, Pakistan. The University had 5 campuses, 13 departments, 9 colleges and over 620 permanent faculty members. To meet the time constraints, a method of probability sampling, multi stage sampling was used. A total of 250 questionnaires were distributed among the selected faculty members and 169 responded back (response rate 67.6%). SPSS 17.0 was used for data analysis. The findings of the study indicated that compensation was positively associated with both teacher's commitment and job satisfaction. Findings of the study also revealed that married and female teachers were more satisfied and committed with their institutions. Similarly satisfaction and commitment level of the teachers increased with the increase in their job experience.[28]

Khalili A. and Asmawi A. (2012) investigated the impact of gender differences on organizational commitment. This research was conducted on randomly selected 108 employees (54 men and 54 women) of LAR Consulting Engineers Company which was a private small and medium enterprise (SME) in Iran. LAR Consulting Engineers (LCE) Company established in 1983 as subsidiary of Ministry of Energy – Tehran Regional water Authority and later in 1986 it became registered private company. The organizational commitment instrument used in this research was adopted from the Allen and Meyer (1990) scale. Based on this scale, three organizational factors (affective commitment, continuance commitment and normative commitment) were evaluated. The findings indicated that men and women had the same level of affective commitment, continuance commitment, and an overall organizational commitment. However results revealed that women have a greater level of normative commitment than men within the SME.[29]

Obalola M., Aduloju K. and Olowokudejo F. (2012) conducted a study on organizational commitment and corporate ethical values: exploring the nexus between employees' psychological contract and firms' ethical behaviour in the Nigerian insurance industry. The respondents of this study were randomly selected through a multi-stage cluster sampling from the list of managers working in the Nigerian insurance industry. It was found that top management support for ethics had the highest correlation ($r = 0.346$, $n = 414$, $p < 0.01$) with organizational commitment. Both dimensions of corporate ethical values were significant predictors of organizational commitment.[30]

Hawass H. H. (2012) conducted a study on committed salesforce: an investigation into personality traits. The purpose of this study was to investigate whether affective and continuance dimensions of organizational commitment were deliberately influenced by a defined set of personality traits. The study applied well-established measurements of organizational commitment and personality traits on a sample of sales representatives in six major Egyptian pharmaceuticals. The findings revealed that organizational commitment was an attitude which was influenced by the sales man's personality traits.[31]

Abdullah and Ramay M. I. (2012) conducted a study on antecedents of organizational commitment of banking sector employees in Pakistan. The aim of this study was to check the association of factors like work environment, job security, pay satisfaction and participation in decision making; with organizational commitment of the employees, working in the banking sector of Pakistan. Two hundred and fifteen (215) responses to questionnaire-based survey were collected from managerial and non-managerial employees, and analyzed. The analysis showed positive correlations between the dependent and independent variables. The relation between job security and organizational commitment was the most significant, indicating that a secure job can yield higher level of commitment. Work environment also had a significant relation with organizational commitment, showing that a healthy and friendly work environment may enhance an employee's commitment towards his work and organization. Pay satisfaction and participation in decision-making had low correlations with organizational commitment. Age and tenure seemed to affect the commitment of employees, with higher commitment shown for higher age and tenure; whereas gender did not show significant change in commitment level of employees.[32]

REFERENCES

1) Sheldon M. E. (1971). Investments, involvements and mechanisms of producing commitments to the organizations. Administrative Sciences Quarterly, Vol. 16, pp. 142-150.

2) Alluto J. A., Hrebiniak L. G., and Alonso R. C. (1973). On operationalizing the concept of commitment. Social Forces, Vol. 51, pp. 448-454.

3) Shoemaker D. J., Snizek W. E., and Bryant C. D. (1977). Toward a further clarification of Becker's side-bet hypothesis as applied to organizational and occupational commitment. Social Forces, Vol. 56, pp. 598-603.

4) Wiener Y. and Vardi Y. (1980). Relationships between job, organization, and career commitments and work outcomes: An integrative approach. Organizational Behavior and Human Performance, Vol. 26, pp. 81-96.

5) Amernic J. H. and Aranya N. (1983) organizational commitment: testing two theories. Industrial Relations, Vol. 38, (2), pp. 319-343.

6) Aranya N., Kushnir T., and Valency A. (1986). Organizational commitment in a male-dominated profession. Human Relations, Vol. 39, pp. 433-448.

7) DeCotiis T. and Summers T. (1987). A path analysis of a model of the antecedents and consequences of organizational commitment. Human Relations, Vol. 40, pp. 445-470.

8) Morrow P. C. and McElroy J. C. (1987). Work commitment and job satisfaction over three career stages. Journal of Vocational Behavior, Vol. 30, pp. 330-346.

9) Angle H. and Perry J. (1991). An empirical assessment of organizational commitment and organizational effectiveness. Administrative Science Quarterly, Vol. 26, pp. 1-14.

10) Dunham R., Grube J. and Castaneda M. (1994). Organizational commitment: The utility of an integrative definition. Journal of Applied Psychology, Vol. 79, pp. 370-380.

11) Cohen A. and Kirchmeyer C. (1995). A multidimensional approach to the relations between organizational commitment and nonwork participation. Journal of Vocational Behavior, Vol. 46, pp. 189-202.

12) Hawkins W. D. (1997). Predictors of affective organizational commitment among high school principals. A Ph.D. thesis, Virginia Polytechnic Institute and State University.

13) Saeed A. (1998). Organizational commitment of teachers in government, K. M. C. and private primary schools of Karachi. A Ph.D. thesis, Hamdard University.

14) Dawley D. D., Stephens R. D. and Stephens D. B. (2005). Dimensionality of organizational commitment in volunteer workers: Chamber of Commerce board members and role fulfillment. Journal of Vocational Behaviour, Vol. 67(3), pp. 511-525.

15) Popoola S.O. (2007). Workplace, biographical and motivation factors affecting organizational commitment of records officers in Nigerian Federal Universities. African Journal of Library Archival and Information Science, Vol. 17 (1), pp. 33-44.

16) Nyengane M. H. (2007). The relationship between leadership style and employee commitment: an exploratory study in an electricity utility of South Africa. A Ph.D. thesis, Rhodes University.

17) Donya A. L. (2007) conducted a study on organizational commitment of senior woman administrators. A Ph.D. thesis, The Florida State University.

18) Khurshid F. (2008). The relationship of personality characteristics with occupational role stress and organizational commitment among university teachers. A Ph.D. thesis, National University of Modern Languages, Islamabad.

19) Kim M., Jones P. and Rodriguez A. (2008). Influence of Work Status on Organizational Commitment and Sport Identity of University Athletic Department Workers. Journal of Issues in Intercollegiate Athletics, Vol. 1, pp. 74-86.

20) Salami S. O. (2008). Demographic and psychological factors predicting organizational commitment among industrial workers. Anthropologist, Vol. 10(1), pp. 31-38.

21) Butt Z. U. (2009). The relationship between occupational stress and organizational commitment in nongovernmental

organizations of Pakistan. National University of Modern Languages, Islamabad.

22) WeiBo Z., Kaur S. and Jun W. (2010). New development of organizational commitment: A critical review (1960 - 2009). African Journal of Business Management, Vol. 4 (1), pp. 12-20.

23) Khan M. R., Ziauddin, Jam F. A. and Ramay M. I. (2010). The impacts of organizational commitment on employee job performance. European Journal of Social Sciences, Vol. 15 (3), pp. 292-298.

24) Baksh A. M. (2010). Organizational commitment of managerial employees: a unified theory and antecedents. A Ph.D. thesis, University of Southern Queensland.

25) Anvari R., Amin S. M., Ahmad U. N., Seliman S., and Garmsari M. (2011). The relationship between strategic compensation practices and affective organizational commitment. Interdisciplinary Journal of Research in Business, Vol. 1 (2), pp.44-55.

26) Bashir M., Jianqiao L., Zhang Y., Ghazanfar F., Abrar M. and Khan M. M. (2011). The relationship between high performance work system, organizational commitment and demographic factors in public sector universities of Pakistan. Interdisciplinary Journal of Research in Business, Vol. 1 (8), pp. 62-71.

27) Akinbode G. A. and Fagbohungbe O. B. (2012). Leadership and organizational factors as predictors of employees'

organizational commitment in Nigeria: an empirical analysis. Business and Management Research, Vol. 1 (2), pp. 69-87.

28) Islam T., Ahmad Z., Ahmed I., Ahmad A., Saeed M. and Muhammad S. K. (2012). Does compensation and demographical variable influence on teachers' commitment and job satisfaction? A study of University of the Punjab, Pakistan. International Journal of Business and Management, Vol. 7 (4), pp. 35-43.

29) Khalili A. and Asmawi A. (2012). Appraising the impact of gender differences on organizational commitment: empirical evidence from a private SME in Iran. International Journal of Business and Management Vol. 7 (5), pp. 100-110.

30) Obalola M., Aduloju K. and Olowokudejo F. (2012). Organizational commitment and corporate ethical values: exploring the nexus between employees' psychological contract and firms' ethical behaviour in the Nigerian insurance industry. Journal of Management and Sustainability, Vol. 2 (1), pp. 43-56.

31) Hawass H. H. (2012). Committed salesforce: An investigation into personality traits. International Journal of Business and Management, Vol. 7 (6), pp. 147-160.

32) Abdullah and Ramay M. I. (2012). Antecedents of organizational commitment of banking sector employees in Pakistan. Serbian Journal of Management, Vol. 7 (1), pp. 89-102.

CHAPTER – V

RESEARCHES RELATING TO THE RELATIONSHIP BETWEEN JOB SATISFACTION AND JOB INVOLVEMENT

Weissenberg and Gruenfeld (1968) investigated the relationship between motivator and hygiene satisfaction variables to job involvement of 96 civil service supervisors. Results of the study were that motivator, but not hygiene satisfaction variables, correlated with job involvement. Weissenberg and Gruenfeld concluded that job involvement can be considered as an important measure of organizational effectiveness that is at least in part, influenced by job satisfaction.[1]

Mushwana and Scotch Eric (1998) investigated the relationship between job involvement and job satisfaction between the traffic officers and bus drivers of the Germiston Transitional Local Council. The results of this study supported the hypotheses that there is no statistically significant difference between the mean test scores of traffic officers and bus drivers in respect of job involvement and job satisfaction and there is no statistically significant correlation between job involvement and job satisfaction.[2]

Joshi G. (1999) studied the relationship between the age, job experience, monthly income and education level of industrial employees of public and private sector with their job involvement and work involvement. The study also investigated reputed the relationship between job satisfaction, job involvement and work involvement. The result revealed that age, job experience and monthly income were significantly associated with their job involvement and work involvement. Employees' monthly income was found to be significant correlated with job satisfaction. The result further revealed that employees' job satisfaction and job involvement were significantly associated. Further the results revealed that work involvement and job satisfaction were not significantly related but had inverse relationship.[3]

YIP Wal-ling (2003) conducted a study which aimed at exploring the job satisfaction and job involvement among the Assistant Social Work Officers in the Social Welfare Department, identifying the predictive factors in determining job satisfaction as well as to find out the relationship between job satisfaction and job involvement. Snowball non-probability sampling method was used and self-administrated questionnaires were distributed to the subjects under study. The results indicated that the respondents were satisfied with and involved in their job while there was a positive relationship between job satisfaction and job involvement. For the predictive factors of job satisfaction, it was found out that all the intrinsic job factors, extrinsic job factors and job characteristics factors were the predicting factors of job satisfaction. Yet, the intrinsic and extrinsic job factors had stronger strength of association with job satisfaction when comparing with the job characteristics factors. Besides, the results suggested that the respondents' nature of servicing unit was correlated with statistical significance to job satisfaction whereas their age, salary, as well as the need to work on extended hours were correlated with statistical significance with job involvement.[4]

Doobree D. (2009) investigated job involvement among bank managers in Mauritius. The sampling frame consisted of 500 bank managers drawn from a stratified sample consisting of junior level and middle level management cadre from the Central Bank, Development Bank of Mauritius, eleven commercial banks with branches scattered over the Island of Mauritius and fourteen offshore banks. It was found that there were no significant relationships between the gender, age, managerial level, educational qualification, background, marital status, number of dependents, length of service and locus of control of bank managers and their job involvement. This study also revealed that there was no significant relationship between job satisfaction of bank managers and their job involvement.[5]

Dogan H. (2009) conducted a comparative study for employee job satisfaction in Aydın Municipality and Nazilli Municipality. The aim of this study was to define the relationships between job satisfaction and the potential variables of pay, promotion, positive affectivity/encouragement, job involvement, potential of rest-day/off-day, relations with co-workers, health facilities, relations with supervisor, training and education facilities, autonomy, physical facilities, reconciliation role of supervisor, procedural justice, tangible aids, office tools, level of role clearness, participation in decisions, management style of supervisor. These municipalities have been chosen for similarities in employee number, city population, and service area. A completed employee questionnaire of 220 was obtained from 127 (35.3%) of Nazilli Municipality's 360 employees, and 93 (18.8%) of Aydın Municipality's 494 employees. It was found that job satisfaction was positively related with job involvement (r = 0.501). All other variables also showed positive relationships with job satisfaction except promotion.[6]

Ishwara P. (2010) examined the determinants of job involvement and job satisfaction among teaching professionals. The present investigation was carried out to measure and assess perceived level of job involvement and job satisfaction among the university teachers working at Post Graduate Departments in the Karnataka State. The sample consisted of 304 teachers (120 Assistant Professors, 94 Associate Professors and 90 Professors) whose average age ranged from 36 to 49 years. To measure and asses job involvement of the teachers, Lodhal and Kejner inventory was administered. Analysis of the data indicated that around 60 per cent of the university teachers perceived and reported to have moderately involved in the job (Mean 75.06 and S.D 6.05). There was no significant difference between in the levels of job involvement among the university teachers i.e. irrespective of cadres all teachers perceived more or less same level of job involvement (The difference is statistically insignificant). As far as the overall job satisfaction (Brayfield and Rothe Model) of the university teachers was concerned, 2/3 of the respondents perceived and reported to have moderate and above moderate levels of overall job satisfaction. Measurement of specific job satisfaction explains the feeling of a respondent for a particular aspect associated with his job and its environment. The teachers in the university perceived and reported less satisfied aspects of the job like mentoring, library facility, clerical assistance, team work (Mean values less than 3.00). On the other hand, the factors of higher fulfillment are work itself, pay, recognition for good work, achievement, research work, status, creativity, responsibility, professional growth, working condition and job security. There is a positive association between overall job satisfaction and specific job satisfaction as well as job satisfaction and job involvement of the university teachers.[7]

Khan K. and Nemati A. R. (2011) investigated impact of job involvement on employee satisfaction: A study based on medical doctors working at Riphah International University Teaching Hospitals in Pakistan. The study was cross sectional. The study is based on the data collected from the medical doctors serving at the Teaching Hospitals of Riphah International University (RIU), Islamabad, namely Pakistan Railway Hospital

(PRH), Rawalpindi, Islamic International Medical Complex (IIMC), Islamabad and Islamic International Dental Complex (IIDC) Islamabad. The sample is a blend of doctors of various disciplines like medicine, surgery and dentistry. The primary objective of this research was to study the impact of job involvement on the level of job satisfaction of doctors serving at the Teaching Hospitals of RIU. This study has empirically demonstrated that job involvement has a significant positive relationship (0.43, $p < 0.01$) with the level of job satisfaction among the selected sample of doctors. The regression analysis indicated that only 19% variance in the dependent variable was explained by the independent variable. This low value indicated that there were other variables which contributed towards job satisfaction of doctors working at Teaching Hospitals of RIU.[8]

REFERENCES

1) Weissenberg P. and Gruenfeld L. W. (1968). Relationship between job satisfaction and job involvement. Journal of Applied Psychology, Vol. 52(6), pp. 469-473.

2) Mushwana and Scotch Eric (1998). The job involvement and job satisfaction between traffic officers and bus drivers. Retrieved from http://hdl.handle.net/10210/5924 on 4th July 2013.

3) Joshi G. (1999). Job satisfaction, job and work involvement among industrial employees: A correlational study. Journal of Indian Academy of Applied Psychology, Vol. 25(1), pp. 79-82.

4) YIP Wal-ling (2003). A study of job satisfaction and job involvement of Assistant Social Work Officers in the Social Welfare Department. A dissertation for the degree of Master of Social Sciences, University of Hong Kong.

5) Doobree D. (2009). Job involvement among bank managers in Mauritius. A Ph. D. thesis, University of Southern Queensland.

6) Dogan H. (2009) conducted a comparative study for employee job satisfaction in Aydın Municipality and Nazilli Municipality. Ege Academic Review, Vol. 9 (2), pp. 423-433.

7) Ishwara P. (2010). Determinants of job involvement and job satisfaction among teaching professionals. Global Journal of Management and Business Research, Vol. 10 (5), pp. 64-74.

8) Khan K. and Nemati A. R. (2011). Impact of job involvement on employee satisfaction: A study based on medical doctors working at Riphah International University Teaching Hospitals in Pakistan. African Journal of Business Management, Vol.5 (6), pp. 2241-2246.

CHAPTER – VI

RESEARCHES RELATING TO THE RELATIONSHIP BETWEEN JOB SATISFACTION AND ORGANIZATIONAL COMMITMENT

Jermier and Berkes (1979) collected data on organizational commitment from over 800 police officers. The researchers were investigating the relationship between job satisfaction and organizational commitment. Findings revealed that employees who were more satisfied with their job had higher levels of organizational commitment.[1]

Cramer D. (1996) studied the relationship between job satisfaction and continuance commitment among professional employees in a British engineering company. This research involved the use of LISREL with latent variable analysis. The two panel study's findings suggested that the relationship between job satisfaction and continuance commitment was false.[2]

Niehoff (1997) conducted a study on the relationship between job satisfaction and organizational commitment among employees at a Catholic university. The study revealed a significant but small correlation existed between job satisfaction and organizational commitment among university employees.[3]

Irving, Coleman and Cooper (1997) investigated the relationship between affective, continuance, and normative commitment and the outcome measures of job satisfaction and turnover intentions. Total participants for the study included 232 employees. Job satisfaction was positively related to both affective and normative commitment. However, it was negatively related to continuance commitment. All three types of commitment were negatively related to turnover intentions, with continuance commitment having the strongest negative relationship.[4]

Busch, Fallan and Peterson (1998) conducted a study to explore and reveal differences in performance indicators among faculty employees of the nursing teacher education, engineering, and business administration programmes in the college sector in Norway. The performance indicators studied were job satisfaction, self efficacy, goal commitment, and organizational commitment. The study revealed a positive correlation between organizational commitment and job satisfaction among faculty employees.[5]

Sagie (1998) reported a high positive correlation between job satisfaction and organizational commitment among 140 clerks in an Israeli municipality.[6]

Al-Aameri (2000) conducted a study to find the relationship between job satisfaction and organizational commitment of nurses in public hospitals in Riyadh City. The result revealed a strong positive relationship between job satisfaction and organizational commitment.[7]

Bull I. H. (2005) conducted a research on the relationship between job satisfaction and organizational commitment amongst high school teachers in disadvantaged areas in the Western Cape. A cross-sectional research method, based on the survey approach was utilized. The population for this research included teachers from 16 high schools in disadvantaged areas in the Western Cape including areas such as: Bridgetown, Hanover Park, Gugulethu, Weltevreden Park and Mitchell's Plain (all classified as previously disadvantaged). Four hundred and fifty (450) teachers were targeted in areas which have been classified as disadvantaged. There was a significant relationship between organizational commitment and job satisfaction ($r = 0.434$, $p < 0.01$). The correlation between job satisfaction and biographical variables (age, job level, tenure, gender and educational level) was found to be significant. The correlation between job satisfaction and organizational commitment except educational level was found to be significant.[8]

Kim W. G., Leong J. K. and Lee Y. (2005) focused on the effects of service orientation on job satisfaction, organizational commitment and intention to leave in a casual dining chain restaurant. Customer focus of employees was negatively associated with job satisfaction, but positively associated with organisation commitment. Job satisfaction was positively and significantly associated with organizational commitment($r = 0.32$, $p < 0.01$), with the reliability coefficients for job satisfaction (0.80) and organizational commitment (0.75) being above the threshold of 0.70 for reliability.[9]

Feinsten A. H. and Vondrasek D. (2006) examined the relationship between the variables of job satisfaction and organizational commitment using a sample of employees working for a restaurant chain. Analysis was carried out using ANOVA and multiple regression analysis. Some of the findings from the sample data were that satisfaction with policies, compensation, working conditions and advancement had a significant relationship to organizational commitment.[10]

Cetin (2006) conducted a study into the relationship between job satisfaction, occupational, and organizational commitment of academics in education faculties at four state universities in Istanbul. The result revealed a strong positive relationship between job satisfaction of academic and their affective and normative commitment to both their organization and occupation.[11]

Tella A., Ayeni C.O. and Popoola S.O. (2007) examined work motivation, job satisfaction, and organizational commitment of library personnel in academic and research libraries in Oyo state, Nigeria. This study used a descriptive survey design. The target population of the study was library personnel in all research and academic libraries in Oyo state, Nigeria. A census of five research and four academic libraries was taken. A total enumeration sampling technique was used to select 200 library personnel. Of these, 82 (41%) were females; while 118 (59%) were males. The research result revealed a positive correlation between work motivation and job satisfaction with coefficient value of r = 0.4056. Motivation correlated with organizational commitment, but the correlation was negative with coefficient value r = - 0.1767. There was a positive correlation between job satisfaction and organizational commitment with coefficient value r = 0.1383. The findings of this study have pointed out some salient issues in the field of librarianship. It is imperative for library management to meet the demands of their personnel to strengthen their motivation, satisfaction, and commitment to minimize turnover. Governments and library management should concentrate on improving the conditions for library personnel.[12]

Huseyin Izgar (2007) conducted a research on job satisfaction of school managers and organizational commitment. In this study, the correlation between school managers' job satisfactions and organizational commitments had been examined. 42 women, 172 men and altogether 214 school managers who work in elementary and secondary schools that are located in Antalya, Karaman, Konya and Icel cities of Turkey during 2005 and 2006 education terms had participated in the research. Data had been collected by using "The Job Satisfaction Survey (JSS)" and "Organizational Commitment Questionnaire". Independent t-test, One-Way ANOVA and Correlation have been used to analyze the data. School managers' job satisfaction had been significantly varied according to gender and management service duration. The level of organizational commitment had significantly been varied according to gender and management service duration. The scores of organizational commitment and job satisfaction had significantly and positively been correlated. The correlation level of job satisfaction had been found 17.4%.[13]

Ho W., Chang C. S., Shih Y. and Liang R. (2007) analyzed the effects of job rotation and role stress among nurses on their job satisfaction and organizational commitment. A sample of 532 nurses provided data which revealed, among other findings, that job rotation could affect their job satisfaction and organizational commitment and that job satisfaction has a positive effect on organizational commitment.[14]

Mosadeghrad A. M., Ferlie E. F. and Rosenberg D. (2008) studied the relationship between job satisfaction, organizational commitment and turnover intention among hospital employees, a sample of 629 employees gave responses to two questionnaires. Among other results of that study, it was revealed that the employees were moderately satisfied with their jobs and committed to their organisations.[15]

Yang and Chang's (2008) study looked at how nursing staff's job satisfaction and organizational commitment levels change when they perform emotional labour. They examined the relationship among emotional labour, job satisfaction and organizational commitment from the perspective of nursing staff. After nursing staff responded to questionnaires, the results revealed, among other findings, that job satisfaction significantly and positively correlated with organizational commitment.[16]

Guleryuz G., Guney S., Aydm E., and Asan O. (2008) conducted a questionnaire survey on the mediating effect of job satisfaction between emotional intelligence and organizational commitment in a sample of nurses. The findings of the study were that emotional intelligence was significantly and positively related to both job satisfaction and organizational commitment. Job satisfaction and organizational commitment were found to have a significant positive correlation.[17]

Xiaohua J. (2008) produced research findings that suggested that that motivation of government employees and their job satisfaction were efficient predictors of their performance. However, public servants' motivation was found to explain more variance in performance than job satisfaction, supporting the idea of a modest correlation between job satisfaction and performance. The findings of the study further revealed that the indirect effects of organizational commitment on performance are achieved by job performance.[18]

Hsiu-Yen Hsu (2009) examined organizational learning culture's influence on job satisfaction, organizational commitment, and turnover intention among research and development professionals in Taiwan during an economic downturn. A quantitative research design using a survey was employed in this study. The target population for this study consisted of R and D professionals from business enterprises in high-tech industries in Taiwan. Seven hundred and seventy-five (775) R and D professionals from the 75 companies were asked to participate in the study. There was a significant and positive correlation among the organizational learning culture, job satisfaction and organizational commitment. All of the correlations were significant with a range of 0.60 to 0.71.[19]

Warsi S., Fatima N. and Sahibzada S. A. (2009) conducted a study focusing on organizational commitment in relation to other variables; among those variables was job satisfaction. The sample was made up of public sector employees. The results obtained from the sample indicated that there was a positive, strong and significant relationship between job satisfaction and organizational commitment. The results also indicated that there was a moderate positive correlation between job involvement and organizational commitment.[20]

Cemile Celik (2009) investigated relationship of organizational commitment and job satisfaction: A field study of tax office employees. The purpose of this study was to examine the relationship between components of organizational commitment and job satisfaction of tax Office employees. This research was performed with the 233 staff (131 male and 102 female) working in a Tax Office in Mersin. Perceptions of the tax Office staff were used as the data in the research. Regarding the scores obtained from normative commitment at the level of $p < 0.05$ significance in

Kruskal Wallis test, a statistically significant difference was identified among job satisfaction levels (p = 0.050). Workers who weren't satisfied with their job had apparently higher normative commitment average. Regarding the scores obtained from affective commitment, a statistically significant difference was identified (p = 0.004). That is, even though workers weren't satisfied with their job, they deem themselves affectively committed to the institute. On the other hand, regarding the scores obtained from continuance commitment, no statistically significant difference was found (p = 0.101).[21]

Gunlu E., Aksarayli M. and Percin N. S. (2010) conducted a study on the relationship between job satisfaction and organizational commitment among hotel managers in Turkey. Basically the study looked at the relationship between job satisfaction and organizational commitment. It also looked at whether there was a significant relationship between the characteristics of the sample, job satisfaction and organizational commitment. The results obtained from this study indicated that extrinsic, intrinsic and general job satisfaction have a significant effect on normative and affective commitment. The findings further suggested that the dimensions of job satisfaction had no significant impact on continuance commitment among the hotel managers.[22]

Azeem S. M. (2010) investigated the nature of relationships of demographic factors (age and job tenure) and job satisfaction facets with organizational commitment. A sample of 128 employees was randomly selected from 5 service organizations in Muscat. Pearson's product moment correlation coefficient and multiple regression analyses were used to analyze the data. The Results of the study showed that the mean values of job satisfaction and organizational commitment were at moderate side. A moderate significant positive relationship was found among job satisfaction facets, demographic factors, and organizational commitment. Supervision, pay, overall job satisfaction, age, and job tenure were the significant predictors of organizational commitment.[23]

Shastri R. K., Mishra K. S. and Sinha A. (2010). The aim of this study was to further our understanding on the relationship of charismatic leadership and organizational commitment in Indian organization. A total of 147 employees from eastern and northern India participated in the study. It was found that with a beta value of 0.38 for charismatic leadership and 0.42 for job satisfaction level reached statistical significance at the 0.001 and was the best significant predictor of organizational commitment. Moreover, the fact that both job satisfaction (0.42, $p < 0.001$) and charismatic leadership (0.38, $p < 0.001$) carried positive beta weights which suggested that positive relationships exist between these two variables and organizational commitment of the employees in organization. Nature of job, with an obtained beta value of only 0.09 was the poorest predictor of organizational commitment.

Length of service and gender of employee also reaches (beta values were 0.27 and 0.23) statistically significant at 0.05 and 0.01 levels, it indicated that organizational commitment of employees was also affected by gender and length of service of employee. It was also concluded that age, educational background and nature of job did not predict organizational commitment based on the sample of employees.[24]

Malik M. E., Nawab S., Naeem B. and Danish R. Q. (2010) conducted a study on job satisfaction and organizational commitment of university teachers in public sector of Pakistan. In this study, descriptive research design was used. The study was carried on teaching faculty working in two public sector universities of Pakistan. One of them was federally chartered university whereas other was provincially (Punjab) chartered university. About 650 survey questionnaires were distributed in October, 2009 by employing diverse modes of communication such as email, in person and post. Multiple follow ups yielded 331 statistically usable questionnaires. Stepwise regression analysis and one sample t-tests were used to confirm the research hypotheses. The findings of the study indicated that the satisfaction with work-itself, quality of supervision and pay satisfaction had significant positive influence on organizational commitment of faculty members. They had high degree of organizational commitment and satisfaction with work-itself, supervision, salary, coworkers and opportunities for promotion.[25]

Ahmad H., Ahmad K. and Shah I. A. (2010) examined the relationship between job satisfaction, job performance attitude towards work and organizational commitment. This study utilized survey data collected from 310 employees of 15 advertising agencies of Islamabad (Pakistan) to test interdependency of job satisfaction and job performance, effect of organizational commitment and attitude towards work on job satisfaction and impact of organizational commitment and attitude towards work on performance. Response patterns, analyzed by gender, education, department, income and age were also discussed. Results showed a weak relation between job satisfaction and performance where as organizational commitment had strong positive relation with performance and attitude towards work had a strong positive relation with job satisfaction. The study identified insignificant impact of organizational commitment on job satisfaction and attitude towards work on job performance.[26]

Sinem Aydogdu and Baris Asikgil (2011) conducted an empirical study of the relationship among job satisfaction, organizational commitment and turnover intention. The sample of this study was conducted from two organizations in Istanbul. Both of these organizations were in private sector, one of these organizations was in production area, the other one was service provider. The sample consisted of total 182 individuals from these two organizations. Since the participation in this study was voluntary, 100 employees in Company X, which was in the production area and 82 employees in Company Y, which was in the service area. The relationship among job satisfaction, organizational commitment and turnover intention were investigated to determine statistically significant relations. The results of the study supported the hypotheses. Job Satisfaction had a significant and positive relationship with three dimensions of organizational commitment and turnover intention had a significant and negative relationship with job satisfaction and organizational commitment.[27]

Loong L. K. (2011) conducted a study was to examine the relationship of job satisfaction, organizational empowerment and trust, career advancement opportunities and moderating effect of gender on organizational commitment. Five broadly hypothesized relationships were tested in a field of study among executives and non-executives serving in retail industry within Klang Valley, Malaysia. Out of 2500 questionnaires posted out to the selected retail outlets within Klang Valley, Malaysia, 983 completed questionnaires were returned of which only 961 were usable (39% return rate) which was considered a very good respond especially in the survey method research. Those retails and respondents that selected in this research paper were the executives and non-executives that engaged their services in multiple branches within Klang Valley, Malaysia. The result of the study showed a positive relationship between organizational commitment with job satisfaction, organizational empowerment and trust, and organizational justice. It also showed that there was a significant relationship between the employees' personal attributes such as gender. The overall result showed that, the higher the organizational commitment level that employees possessed the better performance will be delineated towards their organization.[28]

Eliyana A., Yusuf R. M. and Prabowo K. (2012) aimed to examine about organizational commitment in relation to the job satisfaction factors. Research was conducted on the production employees of PT Jaya Readymix Concrete (JRC) which amounted to 47 people. Analysis techniques used in research was regression analysis between factors of employees' job satisfaction as independent variables, which consisted of ability utilization, compensation, relationship with co-workers, working conditions, recognition and achievement with organizational commitment as dependent variables. Based on the results of the regression analysis of linear regression model equations, we derived a formulation as follows: $Y = -1.012 + 0.184X1 + 0.581X2 + 0.080X3 + 0.118X4 + 0.136X5 + 0.165X6 + e$. Results showed that the job satisfaction factors simultaneously had a significant effect on organizational commitment in JRC with the coefficient of determination (R^2) is 0.967, and that compensation was the dominant variables influencing employee's organizational commitment in the production department at JRC.[29]

Shafaee J., Rahnama A., Alaei A. and Jasour J. (2012) evaluated the impact of organizational structure and job characteristics on job satisfaction and organizational commitment. The main objective of this study was evaluation of the impact of organizational structure and job characteristics on job satisfaction and organizational commitment of employees. In this study statistical society is Parsabad Islamic Azad University employees. The statistical society was of 112 members because statistical society was small thus total statistical society were considered as the sample. A questionnaire was used to collect data. Results of the study suggested that these variables of the organizational structure may effect on job characteristics. Also job characteristics had a positive effect on job satisfaction and job satisfaction had a positive effect on organizational commitment of Parsabad Islamic Azad University employees.[30]

Adekola B. (2012) in his study on the impact of organizational commitment on job satisfaction: a study of employees at Nigerian universities had hypothesized that there is a significant difference in the degree of organizational commitment in public and private universities. Data were collected from 150 employees consisting of academic and administrative and technical staff from Osun State University (Public) and Fountain University (Private) both based in Osun State of Nigeria was used for the study. For sampling, simple random sampling was used. The results revealed that employees in public universities have greater degree of organizational commitment in comparison to private universities. Also, job satisfaction increases or decreases based on increase or decrease in organizational commitment. Obtained results were in the line of the hypotheses. In terms of organizational commitment; a significant difference was noticed between public and private universities. Against expectation, employees of public universities exhibited higher degree of organizational commitment as compared to those of private universities. Most importantly, organizational commitment was being proven as the catalyst for enhancing job satisfaction level of employees.[31]

Hassani S. R., Jalilian O. and Khaleghinezhad G. (2012) studied any relations between job satisfaction dimensions with organizational commitment of personnel at Islamic Azad University- Kermanshah Unit. Sample for this study included all occupied personnel of Islamic Azad University-Kermanshah Unit in 2010. According to the obtained statistics, there were about 239 occupied persons including 63 females and 176 males. It was found that there was a meaningful relation between satisfaction of salary, type of job, job upgrading, supervisor and colleagues and organizational commitment of personnel. The result of this research showed that that job satisfaction was one of the most important problems for managers at executive organizations. This was because any lack of job satisfaction might have great effect on personnel efficiency and might cause a reduction in their work performance. Also it might cause some mental disorders for them.[32]

Karim F. and Rehman O. (2012) studied impact of job satisfaction, perceived organizational justice and employee empowerment on organizational commitment in semi-government organizations of Pakistan. A random sample of 148 employees of Civil Aviation Authority in the cities of Islamabad, Lahore and Karachi was selected. The results of this research showed a strong correlation between organizational commitment and job satisfaction. Similarly strong correlation was observed between organizational commitment and perceived organizational justice.[33]

Namin A. T. (2012) conducted an empirical study on measuring the effect of layoff on job satisfaction and employee commitment: A case study of detergent producer unit. One of the necessary actions in many organizations is to reduce the number of workers in an attempt to restructure business activities. However, layoff could have negative consequences since many employees may decide to leave since they lose their tolerance. The layoff must be accompanied with some supportive plans to reduce stress among the remaining workers and increase their commitment for long-term work. This study considered the effects of layoff on job satisfaction and commitment among the remaining employees of a detergent producer unit. The results indicated that a good supportive program including wage increase, family support, health care plans, etc. could significantly improve employee long-term commitments and it leads to job satisfaction.[34]

Javad E. and Davood G. (2012) studied organizational commitment and job satisfaction of Iranian employees in a firm of services. The purpose of this study was to examine the role job satisfaction on organizational commitments. In this study, data collected from 280 Iranian employees in a firm of services. The present study employed a questionnaire survey approach to collect data for testing the research hypotheses. Relevant statistical analytical techniques including regression for analysis was then used. The results indicated that all three factors of Job satisfaction (Promotions, Personal relationships, and Favorable conditions of work) had positive and significant effects on organizational commitments. The main contribution of the study was to provide empirical evidence about the impact of job satisfaction on organizational commitments.[35]

Daneshfard C. and Ekvaniyan K. E. (2012) conducted a study on organizational commitment and job satisfaction in Islamic Azad University. The main purpose of this study was the comparison job satisfaction and organizational commitment in employees, managers and members of the delegation in Islamic Azad University of Kogiluyeh and Boyer Ahmad province. Using stratified sampling method 223 people (23 manager, 105 employees, and 95 faculty member) were selected randomly. The result of this study showed that the relationship between employee job satisfaction and employee organizational commitment is direct and significant. There was a significant difference in job satisfaction among managers, faculty members and employees, whereas there was insignificant difference in organizational commitment among manager, faculty members and employees.[36]

REFERENCES

1) Jermier J. and Berkes L. (1979). Leader behavior in a police command bureaucracy: A closer look at the quasi-military model. Administrative Science Quarterly, Vol. 24, pp. 1-23.

2) Cramer D. (1996). Job satisfaction and organizational continuance commitment: A two-wave panel study. Journal of Organizational Behavior, Vol. 17(4), pp. 389-400.

3) Niehoff, R. L. (1997). Job satisfaction, organizational commitment, and individual and organizational mission values congruence: Investigating the relationships. Paper presented at the Annual Convention of the National Catholic Educational Association 94th Minneapolis, April 1-4 1997.

4) Irving, P., Coleman, D., and Cooper, C. (1997). Further assessments of a three-component model of occupational commitment: Generalizability and differences across occupations. Journal of Applied Psychology, Vol. 82(3), pp. 444-452.

5) Busch T., Fallan L., and Peterson A. (1998). Disciplinary differences in job satisfaction and organizational commitment among faculty employees in Norwegian colleges: An empirical assessment of indicators of performance. Quality in Higher Education, Vol. 4(2), pp. 137-157.

6) Sagie A. (1998). Employee absenteeism, organizational commitment, and job satisfaction: Another look. Journal of Vocational Behaviour, Vol. 52(2), pp. 156-171.

7) Al-Aameri A. S. (2000). Job satisfaction and organizational commitment for nurses. Saudi Medical Journal, Vol. 21 (6), pp. 531-535.

8) Bull I. H. (2005). The relationship between job satisfaction and organizational commitment amongst high school teachers in disadvantaged areas in the Western Cape. Mini thesis of M. A., University of the Western Cape.

9) Kim W. G., Leong J. K. and Lee Y. (2005). Effects of service orientation on job satisfaction, organizational commitment, and intention of leaving in a casual dining chain restaurant. International Journal of Hospitality Management, Vol. 24 (2), pp. 171-193.

10) Feinsten A. H. and Vondrasek D. (2006). A study of the relationship between job satisfaction and organizational commitment among restaurant employees. Journal of Hospitality, Tourism and Leisure, Vol. 6(3), pp. 1-26.

11) Cetin M. O. (2006). The relationship between job satisfaction, occupational and organizational commitment of academics. The Journal of American Academy of Business, Vol. 8(1), pp. 78-88.

12) Tella A., Ayeni C.O. and Popoola S.O. (2007). Work motivation, job satisfaction, and organizational commitment of library personnel in academic and research libraries in Oyo state, Nigeria. Library Philosophy and Practice, pp. 1-16.

13) Huseyin I. (2007). A research on job satisfaction of school managers and organizational commitment. Georgian

Electronic Scientific Journal: Education Science and Psychology, Vol. 2(11), pp. 3-11.

14) Ho W., Chang C. S., Shih Y. and Liang R. (2007). Effects of job rotation and role stress among nurses on job satisfaction and organizational commitment. BMC Health Services Research, Vol. 6 (1), pp. 1-10.

15) Mosadeghrad A. M., Ferlie E. F. and Rosenberg D. (2008). A study of the relationship between job satisfaction and, organizational commitment and turnover intention among hospital employees. Health Service Management Research, Vol. 21 (4), pp. 211-227.

16) Yang F. and Chang C. (2008). Emotional labour, job satisfaction and organizational commitment amongst clinical nurses: A questionnaire survey. International Journal of Nursing Studies, Vol. 45 (6), pp.18-27.

17) Guleryuz G., Guney S., Aydm E., and Asan O. (2008). The mediating effect of job satisfaction between emotional intelligence and organizational commitment of nurses: A questionnaire survey. International Journal of Nursing Studies, Vol. 45 (11), pp. 1625-1635.

18) Xiaohua J. (2008). An empirical study on public service motivation and the performance of government employees in China. Canadian Social Science, Vol. 4 (2), pp. 10-28.

19) Hsiu-Yen Hsu (2009). Organizational learning culture's influence on job satisfaction, organizational commitment, and turnover intention among research and development

professionals in Taiwan during an economic downturn. A Ph. D. thesis, University Of Minnesota, China.

20) Warsi S., Fatima N. and Sahibzada S. A. (2009). Study on the relationship between organizational commitment and its determinants among private sector employees of Pakistan. International Review of Business Research Papers, Vol. 5 (3), pp. 399-410.

21) Cemile C. (2009). Relationship of organizational commitment and job satisfaction: A field study of tax office employees. A Ph.D. thesis, Mersin University, Turkey.

22) Gunlu E., Aksarayli M. and Percin N. S. (2010). Job satisfaction and organizational commitment of hotel managers in Turkey. International Journal of Contemporary Hospitality Management, Vol. 22 (5), pp. 693-717.

23) Azeem S. M. (2010). Job satisfaction and organizational commitment among employees in the Sultanate of Oman. Psychology, Vol. 1, pp. 295-299.

24) Shastri R. K., Mishra K. S. and Sinha A. (2010). Charismatic leadership and organizational commitment: An Indian perspective. African Journal of Business Management, Vol. 4(10), pp. 1946-1953.

25) Malik M. E., Nawab S., Naeem B. and Danish R. Q. (2010). Job satisfaction and organizational commitment of university teachers in public sector of Pakistan. International Journal of Business and Management, Vol. 5(6), pp. 17-26.

26) Ahmad H., Ahmad K. and Shah I. A. (2010). Relationship between job satisfaction, job performance attitude towards work and organizational commitment. European Journal of Social Sciences, Vol. 18(2), pp. 257-267.

27) Sinem Aydogdu and Baris Asikgil (2011). An empirical study of the relationship among job satisfaction, organizational commitment and turnover intention. International Review of Management and Marketing, Vol. 1 (3), pp. 43-53.

28) Loong L. K. (2011). The impact of organizational commitment among executives in retail industry, Klang Valley (Malaysia). The 2nd International Research Symposium in Service Management Yogyakarta, Indonesia.

29) Eliyana A., Yusuf R. M. and Prabowo K. (2012). The influence of employee's job satisfaction factors on organizational commitment. American Journal of Economics, Special Issue, pp. 141-144.

30) Shafaee J., Rahnama A., Alaei A. and Jasour J. (2012). Evaluation of the impact of organizational structure and job characteristics on job satisfaction and organizational commitment. Journal of Basic and Applied Scientific Research, Vol. 2(3), pp. 2329-2335.

31) Adekola B. (2012). The impact of organizational commitment on job satisfaction: A study of employees at Nigerian universities. International Journal of Human Resource Studies, Vol. 2 (2), pp. 1-17.

32) Hassani S. R., Jalilian O. and Khaleghinezhad G. (2012). Any relations between job satisfaction dimensions with organizational commitment of personnel at Islamic Azad University- Kermanshah Unit. Journal of Basic and Applied Scientific Research, Vol. 2(2), pp. 1114-1119.

33) Karim F. and Rehman O. (2012). Impact of job satisfaction, perceived organizational justice and employee empowerment on organizational commitment in semi-government organizations of Pakistan. Journal of Business Studies Quarterly 2012, Vol. 3(4), pp. 92-104.

34) Namin A. T. (2012). An empirical study on measuring the effect of layoff on job satisfaction and employee commitment: A case study of detergent producer unit. Management Science Letters, Vol. 2, pp. 213-220.

35) Javad E. and Davood G. (2012). Organizational commitment and job satisfaction. ARPN Journal of Science and Technology, Vol. 2 (2), pp. 85-91.

36) Daneshfard C. and Ekvaniyan K. E. (2012). Organizational commitment and job satisfaction in Islamic Azad University. Interdisciplinary Journal of Contemporary Research in Business, Vol. 3 (9), pp. 168-181.

CHAPTER – VII

RESEARCHES RELATING TO THE RELATIONSHIP BETWEEN JOB INVOLVEMENT AND ORGANIZATIONAL COMMITMENT

Mathieu J. E. and Zajac D. M. (1990) conducted a review and meta-analysis of the antecedents, correlates and consequences of organizational commitment. The study indicated that organizational commitment was positively related to employee motivation and job involvement and negatively related to absenteeism and turnover.[1]

Randall D. M. and Cote J. A. (1991) investigated interrelationships of work commitment constructs. Strong relationships have been found between job involvement and organizational commitment and job involvement and career salience. In addition, job involvement was significantly influenced by the protestant work ethic. Work group attachment, however, appeared to influence organizational commitment only through job involvement.[2]

Huselid M. A. and Day N. E. (1991) conducted a study to examine the hypothesis that organizational commitment and job involvement interact in the prediction of turnover. The presence of a commitment–involvement interaction was tested in three estimation models with data obtained from 138 supervisors.

Identical models estimated with logistic regression provided no support for the presence of a commitment–involvement interaction. It is concluded that results obtained with linear techniques are a function of an inappropriate estimation procedure when the dependent variable is binary. The potential impact of the widespread use of linear estimation procedures in turnover research was discussed.[3]

Knoop (1995) investigated the relationships among a cluster of attitudes toward work and the job using a sample of 171 nurses. The hypothesis was that involvement in work, commitment to the employing organisation and overall satisfaction with the job would be significantly correlated. The results indicated the degree of the relationship between commitment and job involvement was moderately high.[4]

Cohen (1996) investigated the relationship between affective, continuance, and normative commitment and the following other types of commitment: work involvement, job involvement, and career commitment. Findings revealed that affective commitment was more highly correlated with all the other types of commitment. In other words, employees who remained with the organization because they wanted to were more likely to exhibit higher levels of commitment to their work, their job, and their career.[5]

Lahai M. M. (1997) investigated organizational commitment, job satisfaction and job performance among operators of selected electrical and electronic industries in Klang valley, Malaysia. The primary purpose of this study was to study organizational commitment and job satisfaction and their relationships with job performance among operators of selected electrical and electronic industries in Klang valley, Malaysia. The study was carried out in the industrial areas of Nilai, Ulu Klang and Bangi in Malaysia amongst 426 randomly selected operators in six electronics and electrical industries. The impact of the differential relationships between operators' organizational commitment and their job performance was explored using job satisfaction variables in the Herzberg's Two-Factor Motivation theory as intervening variables. Findings of the study revealed that: level of job performance of the operators was high, the operators' level of commitment and overall job satisfaction were related to their job performance, the influence of organizational commitment on job performance was mediated by overall job satisfaction and the two work related attitudes, organizational commitment and job satisfaction did not appear to be distinct work attitudes.[6]

Dauftuar C. N. and Anjali (1997) explored the influence of occupational stress, organizational commitment and job involvement and personality of lower and middle level managers working in electrical manufacturing company in western India. Result revealed significant positive correlation between job involvement and several areas of occupational stress, organizational commitment and personality types.[7]

Sjoberg and Sverke (2000) conducted a study on the interactive effect of job involvement and organizational commitment on job turnover in a Swedish Emergency Hospital. It was found that organizational commitment and job involvement are significantly positively correlated. It was also found that nurses with a higher level of job involvement and organizational commitment had significantly less unexcused absences than nurses with lower levels of job involvement and organizational commitment.[8]

Chin-Chih Ho (2006) investigated the relationships between work values, job involvement and organizational commitment among Taiwanese nurses. This study investigated the relationship between work values, job involvement and organizational commitment in a sample of 1047 Taiwanese nurses from Taiwan. The study utilized a cross-sectional survey design. The sample consisted of Registered Nurses (RNs) (N = 1,047) recruited from a convenience sample in nine regional and teaching hospitals in Taiwan. The results of the study showed that work values were positively related to job involvement and organizational commitment, and job involvement was positively related to organizational commitment. Subsequent analyses revealed that job involvement could play an important role in mediating the relationship between work values and organizational commitment, and that establishing a higher level of job involvement among employees may be more important than focusing only on organizational commitment. It was further anticipated that improving various work-related attitudes would result in reduced turnover and absenteeism and more effective organisations.[9]

Hung L. M. (2008) conducted a research on how training influences administrative staff job involvement and organizational commitment. This research was based on a survey that took random sampling of a population of the administrative staff from a university of technology in the North in December 2007, where 140 questionnaires were distributed, 108 were valid return, and the return rate was 77.1%. With job involvement as an independent variable and organizational commitment as a dependent variable, a regression analysis was conducted to prove its strength with R^2 of 51.3%. Job involvement had significant positive influence on organizational commitment ($r = 0.7261$, $p = 0.000$). This finding supported the hypothesis that job involvement has positive influence on organizational commitment. It was also found that training has significant positive influence on job involvement ($r = 0.541$, $p = 0.000$) and organizational commitment ($r = 0.574$, $p = 0.000$).[10]

Uygur and Kilic (2009) studied the level of organizational commitment and job involvement of the personnel at Central Organizational, Ministry of Health, in Turkey. Questionnaires were distributed to a total of 210 subjects. Of this number, 180 (86%) returned the questionnaires and of these, 168 were found to be useable. A significant positive correlation was found between organizational commitment and job involvement (r = 0.44).[11]

Khan T. I., Jam F. A., Akbar A., Khan M. B. and Hijazi S. T. (2010) conducted a study on job involvement as predictor of employee commitment: evidence from Pakistan. Data was collected through personally administered questionnaires. For this purpose, data was collected from 11 different public and private sector organizations in Pakistan. Total 260 questionnaires were distributed and 228 questionnaires (response rate of 87.6 %) filled in were received back. Among 228 questionnaires, 211 questionnaires found completely filled in by all aspects. So useable sample data was 211 with response rate of 81%. This study highlighted the effect of job involvement on three types of commitments i.e. affective commitment, Continuance commitment and normative commitment. Job involvement showed the positive relationships with affective commitment (r = 0.59, p < 0.01), continuous commitment (r = 0.34, p < .01) and normative commitment (r = 0.59, p < 0.01).[12]

Biswas S. (2011) investigated psychological climate and affective commitment as antecedents of salespersons' job involvement. The objective of this paper was to explore the relationship between psychological climate and affective commitment as predictors of sales person's level of job performance through the latter's level of job involvement and job satisfaction. For this purpose, a survey instrument was administered to sales and marketing executives and their supervisors from various organizations in India. These organizations were randomly selected from various databases such as Yellow Pages Business Directory, CMIE (Centre for Monitoring Indian Economy) database, and so on. Data thus obtained from the sample (N = 357) was investigated through multivariate statistical techniques. There was a positive relationship between salesperson's affective commitment and his/her level of job involvement.[13]

Ekmekci A. K. (2011) conducted a study on involvement and commitment of employees in Turkey. This study aimed to explore the relationship between employees' job involvement and their feeling of organizational commitment. For that aim, the survey was performed among the employees currently working at two multinational companies in Turkey. The survey data that was collected from 210 questionnaires were analyzed and evaluated. Within the analysis, it was seen that the job involvement perceptions of the employees in Turkey had an effect on their organizational commitment. The demographical factors were examined in terms of their impact on the relationship between employees' job involvement and organizational commitment.[14]

REFERENCES

1) Mathieu J. E. and Zajac D. M. (1990). A review and meta-analysis of the antecedents, correlates and consequences of organizational commitment. Psychological Bulletin, Vol. 108, pp. 171-194.

2) Randall D. M. and Cote J. A. (1991). Interrelationships of work commitment construct. Work and Occupations, Vol. 18, pp. 194-211.

3) Huselid M. A. and Day N. E. (1991). Organizational commitment, job involvement and turnover: A substantive and methodological analysis. Journal of Applied Psychology, Vol. 76 (3), pp. 380-391.

4) Knoop R. (1995). Relationships among job involvement, job satisfaction, and organizational commitment for nurses. Journal of Psychology, Vol. 129(6), pp. 643- 650.

5) Cohen A. (1996). On the discriminant validity of the Meyer and Allen measure of organizational commitment: How does it fit with the work commitment construct? Educational and Psychological Measurement, Vol. 56, pp. 494-503.

6) Lahai M. M. (1997). Organizational commitment, job satisfaction and job performance among operators of selected electrical and electronic industries in Klang valley, Malaysia. A Ph.D. thesis, Universiti Putra Malaysia.

7) Daftuar C. N. and Anjali (1997). Occupational stress, organizational commitment and job involvement in Sattva

Rajas and Tamas personality types. Journal of the Indian Academy of Applied Psychology, Vol. 15(1), pp. 44-52.

8) Sjoberg A., and Sverke M. (2000). The interactive effect of job involvement and organizational commitment on job turnover revisited: A note on the mediating role of turnover intention. Scandinavian Journal of Psychology, Vol. 41, pp. 247-252.

9) Chin-Chih Ho (2006) A study of the relationships between work values, job involvement and organizational commitment among Taiwanese nurses. A Ph.D. thesis, Queensland University of Technology, Australia.

10) Hung L. M. (2008) conducted a research on how training influences administrative staff job involvement and organizational commitment. The Journal of Human Resource and Adult Learning, Vol. 4 (2), pp. 115-121.

11) Uygur A., and Kilic G. (2009). A study into organizational commitment and job involvement: an application towards the personnel in the central organisation for ministry of health in Turkey. Ocean Journal of Applied Sciences, Vol. 2(1), pp. 121-134.

12) Khan T. I., Jam F. A., Akbar A., Khan M. B. and Hijazi S. T. (2010) conducted a study on job involvement as predictor of employee commitment: evidence from Pakistan. International Journal of Business and Management, Vol. 6 (4), pp. 252-262.

13) Biswas S. (2011). Psychological climate and affective commitment as antecedents of salespersons' job involvement. Management Insight, Vol. VII (2), pp. 1-8.

14) Ekmekci A. K. (2011) conducted a study on involvement and commitment of employees in Turkey. Journal of Public Administration and Policy Research, Vol. 3(3), pp. 68-73.

www.ingramcontent.com/pod-product-compliance
Lightning Source LLC
Chambersburg PA
CBHW060351190526
45169CB00002B/565